Nonstop
NETWORKING

Nonstop
NETWORKING

HOW TO IMPROVE YOUR LIFE, LUCK, AND CAREER.

Andrea R. Nierenberg

Capital Books, Inc.

Sterling, Virginia

CAPITAL
BOOKS, INC.

Capital Books, Inc.
P.O. Box 605
Herndon, Virginia 20172-0605

ISBN 1-892123-92-4   (alk. paper)

Library of Congress Cataloging-in-Publication Data
Nierenberg, Andrea.
   Nonstop networking : how to improve your life,
     luck and career / Andrea Nierenberg.—
  1st ed.
     p. cm.
   Includes index.
   ISBN 1-892123-92-4
    1. Business networks. 2. social networks.
     3. Career development. I. Title.
  HD69.S8 N54 2002
  650.1'3—de21   2002072071587

Printed in the United States of America on acid-free paper that
meets the American National Standards Institute Z39-48
Standard.

First Edition

10 9 8 7 6 5 4

To my dear mother, Molly, who has always been my mentor, adviser, and best friend—and even though you say you don't know many people, you really know the whole state of Florida!

And to my wonderful father, Paul—you taught me all the life lessons shared in this book. I know you're looking down from heaven at me and smiling—and as you would say, "Hang right in there." I am, Daddy, and I love you!

I love you both! Thank you.

Contents

Nonstop NETWORKING

When I started to write this book, I struggled with the word networking. At the time, the economy was in a slump and many people had lost their jobs. Some of them, on the well-intentioned advice of career counselors and others, were frantically networking to find a new job. I saw a lot of "negative networking." People were calling long forgotten connections and asking—or in some cases even demanding—information interviews, job referrals, and references. My thoughts about this "negative networking" practice appeared in national media such as *The New York Times*, *The Wall Street Journal*, and *Fortune Online*. This was definitely not networking the way I thought it should be.

Networking is one of the most overused and misunderstood words in our vocabulary today. The dictionary defines networking as "the exchange of information or services among individuals, groups, or institutions." What is left

unsaid in the dictionary definition is the commonly accepted purpose of networking, which is to find a new job, locate new customers, obtain funds to start a new business, or make contacts within your organization to facilitate a project.

Yes, networking is certainly all of that; however, I think of networking in a much larger context. To me, networking is the process of developing and maintaining quality relationships that are mutually beneficial. This process is ongoing—nonstop. The relationships that come of it are connections that can last a lifetime. The result is life enrichment and the empowerment to achieve your life goals.

For me, networking is a way of life. Understanding and learning to network effectively has served me well. Everyday, I realize that my business has grown because of the many connections I have made and continue to make through life. At this point, I have over 2,500 contacts who will answer the phone when I call or call me back. People often say to me, "How did you come to know all these people?" or "How do you stay in touch with so many?" I will show you how in this book. You will learn how to develop a system that works best and is productive for you. You can use my system as a model to develop your own network of contacts.

Where did I learn my networking lessons? Much of it I owe to my wonderful father. In going through his things after his death, my mother and I came across this list of life lessons that he had written down. If you had known him, you would recognize that he lived these everyday. He would always say to me, "Hang right in there and give everyone you meet a smile and a handshake!"

Here is his list:

- Listen with your inner ear. Hear what is said with the heart, rather than what is said with words.
- Listen to the concerns of others.
- Know when it is important just to listen.
- Communication is hard work.
  - Hone your skills.
  - State your thoughts clearly and briefly.
  - Remember to smile, not scowl.
  - Above all, be reasonable and understanding.
  - Be interesting and interested.
  - Be friendly and enthusiastic.
- Have a sense of humor.
- Be human.
- Laugh and grin.

These simple yet effective guiding principles have shaped my life. From these and from my own experience, I have developed the techniques you will read about in this book.

In keeping with my belief to be a resource for others, I want to share these principles, techniques, and stories. I want to show you how they have worked for me, my friends, colleagues, and the many folks who have attended my seminars. I hope you will enjoy, use, and most of all, profit from these words.

Andrea Nierenberg

Acknowledgments

This is the hardest page for me to write. There are so many people who I want to thank personally and give credit for making me a better networker and, more importantly, a better person. I could fill up a whole book letting those people know how I feel about them. This book has been a work-in-progress for about 20 years. It's the result of learning over a lifetime from so many wonderful people.

First and foremost, my thanks to Judy Karpinski, my editor, role model, collaborator, and friend. Without her guidance, help and belief in me, this book clearly would still only be in my mind and not down on paper. To her, I owe all my appreciation.

I also want to thank Tom Ciesielka who is my publicist and head cheerleader. For five years now, he has been helping me grow and succeed and get my name out there. I could never do it without his help.

Mostly, thanks to my wonderful partner, Jon Lambert. He's given me much inner strength and told me all along I could do it. He has been my "rock."

My dear friend Lois Geller is a role model to me in so many ways. My thanks to her for always being there to listen, laugh, or whatever.

My brother Richard and sister Meredith have both taught me so much about relationships and how we each grow from the love of each other.

A huge thanks goes to the wonderful team at Capital Books—Kathleen Hughes, Jane Graf, and Kristen Gustafson. Thank you all for your support and belief in me.

Special thanks also go to: Elaine Pofeldt, Skip Berry, Jeri Sedlar, Rick Miners, Mike Guarini, Chris Heide, Max Bartko, Ken Karpinski, Trudy and Bill Mitchell, Florence Stone, George Salovich, and William Anderson.

Thanks to all for your support, help, and friendship.

Before you begin this book, take a minute to answer these questions:

- How did you find out about your current (or any previous) job?
- How did you meet your spouse?
- How did you choose your neighborhood?
- How do you decide on a vacation spot and accommodations?
- How did you get your last promotion?
- How do you find clients for your business?
- How did you find your doctor, dentist, accountant, day care provider, health club, or favorite restaurant?

Introduction

When you sought advice from people you knew, when someone introduced you to a person who could help you, or when someone championed your cause, you were networking. Have you done the same for others? If so, you were networking. You may not have realized it, but that is the essence of networking.

What you may lack is a systematic approach to networking, a way of life that will help you draw upon the vast number of people with whom you come in contact, by choice or by chance.

In this book, I will show you that networking is simply a way of life. I will teach you how to make the connections, build the relationships, and create a system that will improve your life, luck, and career.

Chapter 1

What Is Networking?

Does the word networking scare you or, even worse, make you cringe? Many people feel that way. Maybe that is why you shy away from the very skill that can help you professionally and personally.

I have a friend who is a great photographer. Her pictures really give true meaning to the phrase "a picture is worth a thousand words." She captures the essence of her subject in each photograph. Yet, she puts off starting her own photography business. As she says "I don't feel ready yet." I think she is fearful of getting out there and building the relationships that will help her grow her business. In other words, she is scared of networking.

You Need to Know How to Network Effectively

Even if the word networking does make you cringe, you know you need to develop this skill

"Networking" Is One of the Most Overused and Misunderstood Words in Common Vocabulary Today

When you hear the word networking what comes to mind?

- Getting something from someone else?
- Using others?
- Coercion?
- Manipulation?

Or...

- Enrichment
- Empowerment
- The chance to learn something new
- An opportunity to meet interesting people
- The best method to achieve a professional or personal goal

Networking is the process of developing and maintaining quality relationships that enrich your life and empower you to achieve your goals.

to be successful. The old saying, "It's not what you know but who you know" is true more than ever in today's competitive world. It is most often the "who you know" that leads you to the next job, new client, funding for your business, successful project in your company, or whatever you may be looking for in life, professionally or personally.

My friend the photographer knows all this. She is a well-educated, competent, professional woman. She has many contacts from her previous career as a marketing manager and knows the value of marketing one's self. Like many of us in the wake of current events such as 9-11, she wants very badly to achieve goals that have become even more important to her. She knows she has to overcome her resistance to networking, yet she can come up with a million and one excuses not to network.

When I started this book, I asked her to share some of her reactions to "networking" with me. Do any of these sound familiar to you?

- I'm basically a shy person.

- I'm uncomfortable starting a conversation with a stranger.

- I don't know how to keep a conversation going, or how to gracefully break away when it is time to move on.

- I'm embarrassed to ask someone for a favor.

- I'm a private person—when I get on a plane or train, the last thing I want to do is chat with the person next to me!

- I'm busy—I hardly have enough time in my life for the people and activities I really care about: family, friends, my kid's soccer games and recitals, or taking a class.

- I don't care for the type of people who call themselves "networkers." I think they are only interested in getting something from me.

- I don't know how to keep track of my contacts. My address book is a mess, and I don't have a PDA or the right software on my computer.

- I haven't followed through with the contacts I've managed to make; therefore, when I do need some information or help, I'm reluctant to make the call.

I can also relate to these. Networking comes easy for me now, but it wasn't always so. At one point in my life, I was very shy. When I first moved to New York City, I knew no one except my grandparents, and now, many years later, I have a database of over 2,500 contacts that is still growing. I soon found out that networking was the way I could enrich and empower myself. Early on in my career, I developed this basic theory about networking, which is, the opposite of networking is <u>not</u> working. In other words, if I am not making connections and nurturing the relationships I have developed, I am simply "not working."

You Already Have the Resources You Need

I once heard that we will all know at least 250 people during the course of our lifetimes through our jobs, social activities, religious affiliations, neighborhoods, clubs, and other organizations. This number can multiply when you realize that each of these people can help you by influencing some of the 250 people they know, just as you can help them by influencing those you know. For example, I once met someone in a workshop who introduced me to his brother who subsequently hired me for an extensive project. Now I could have spent forever calling this person just trying to get an appointment; however, with an introduction from someone who already believed in me, I was able to get an appointment right away, give my presentation, and ultimately land the job.

I get upset when I hear someone say, "I need a new job, so I better start networking." Or, "I only network at certain meetings or events." Why not make networking part of your everyday life? In fact, every time you meet someone new it is an opportunity to learn new things that will enrich and enhance your life.

I like to think of networking as the ongoing process of creating connections and nurturing relationships that benefit both parties over time. You will see as we go through this journey together that it is a process you can start anytime and anywhere in your life. Truth is, you may already be doing it and not know it.

I know someone who is the ultimate networker, yet he has no idea that he is networking. He just seems to know people who can help him and he in turn helps them. He always says, "I have a buddy who (fill in the blank)" for everything. Here is how Bob, the ultimate networker, came to be driving a classic BMW for the unbelievable price of $3,000. (Yes, you read that right!) Bob bought a vintage BMW at an auto auction, which he found out about through a "buddy." He paid a little less than $3,000 cash. The car had a great engine but the body was in bad shape. He did not worry because he had another "buddy" who knew about a BMW with a great body but with a bad engine. He ended up buying that car also—for "practically nothing." He then took both cars to a third "buddy" of his, a mechanic, who exchanged the engines. Now Bob is driving around in his "new" BMW—thanks to networking!

Building Relationships and Reaching Your Potential

You can meet people and network anyplace, anytime. Networking is a "nonstop" process; it is just living your life, connecting with people, and making things happen. Building the relationships you need to reach your potential is easier than you think. I look at it as a simple 5-step process.

1. **Meet people.** Welcome opportunities to meet new people, and re-connect with those you already know.

2. **Listen and learn.** Everybody likes to talk about themselves. When you listen, you will learn who they are, what is important to them, how you can help them, and how they can help you.

3. **Make connections.** Help people connect with others you know who can help them.

4. **Follow up.** If you promise to do something, keep your promise and do it in a timely manner.

5. **Stay in touch.** After an initial period of contact, if a result does not materialize, most people will just move on. Here is where my networking system really "works" for successful networkers. These folks find ways to stay in touch and continue to build relationships. Why? Because their goal is to build a network of long-lasting, mutually beneficial relationships, not just to get an immediate "result."

The simple yet effective system I developed and teach in my networking seminars focuses on these five steps. It is different from other systems in that it is based on building long-lasting relationships, instead of techniques to use in the short term to get a new job, win a contract, or get a promotion. Many of my seminar attendees have told me they had given up on networking because they thought it was only about handing out business cards and asking for referrals. They are pleasantly surprised when they discover and practice the system you will learn about in this book.

What You Will Learn in This Book

In Chapter 2, I start right out with twelve techniques to use when you meet new people, the first step of the networking process. I will show you how to start a conversation, keep it going, learn about others, and have a way to follow up. I'll give you a way to sell yourself with a 30-second infomercial that is so fun and easy you will use it all the time with great results. I'll even give you some "exit strategies" to use when you want to end a conversation. I will ease any anxieties about meeting lots of people by showing you how to set realistic goals for yourself when attending networking events.

In the next chapter we'll talk about the types of people you will want to have in your network. Most people will be pleasantly surprised to learn that these are folks you already know, or can easily meet through connections you already have. You will also discover that you do not have to give up your life to network; in fact, you can enrich your life by creating and developing connections.

For those you of who think you are shy and introverted—and that is most of us, at least at one point in our life—there is a chapter of networking tips just for you.

In the next two chapters, I will show you how to expand your network and keep it growing by staying in touch. Then, because I have seen so many instances of what I call "negative networking," I've included a chapter on Networking Etiquette.

There is even a chapter about how to organize and keep track of your network database. My system is simple; it works just as well on 3- x -5 index cards as it does on MS Outlook™, which is the software I use.

Finally, to tie it all together in the last chapter, I asked some of my clients, attendees of my seminars, and friends to share their networking success stories based on my networking system. There you will find out what my photographer friend did when she finally started her business and how she is using her network to build relationships that will help her achieve her goals.

There is no magic formula to my system of networking. All it takes is a positive attitude about building relationships and a willingness to learn and practice the techniques. As you read this book and put my techniques into practice, you too will improve your life, luck, and career as you meet and develop relationships with the people who can help you achieve your goals.

Now let's take a look at some techniques for networking success you can use at your next networking event.

Chapter 2

Techniques for Networking Success

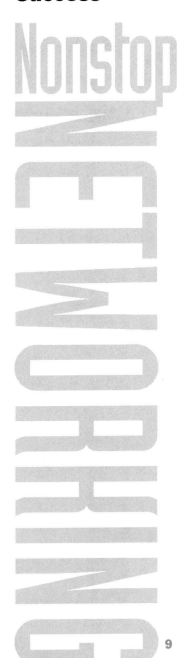

"Let's network," the CEO said. "After Andrea speaks, we'll have an opportunity to get to know each other better!" I was the keynote speaker at the company luncheon and as I looked out into the audience, I could see people's reaction to their CEO's words. Members of the audience immediately broke out in a sweat.

Why did the idea of networking make them so uncomfortable? Perhaps no one had encouraged them to network before. Many within the group may have felt they needed "permission" to walk up to someone who headed another department, introduce themselves, and begin a conversation. True, the CEO gave them his permission, but somehow this was not enough to make them comfortable. Maybe another problem was that they did not know how to network. This created doubts such as,

"How do I begin?", "What if I look like a fool in front of senior management?", and "What are they thinking of me?"

How would you have felt if you had been in their place? How do you feel at any gathering when you are told you have fifteen minutes to "network" before the meeting begins? What are you thinking when you attend a "networking" event at a convention, business meeting, or seminar? What is your attitude when you join an association, trade group, or interest group?

Do any or all of the following thoughts run through your mind?

- How do I approach another person and introduce myself?
- How do I keep the conversation going?
- What if I'm the only new person and everyone else knows each other? Will they think I'm intruding?
- How do I break away from someone so I can keep on mingling?

You are not alone. Many folks who attend my seminars and workshops express these feelings about networking events. It is hard to break old habits. When you are not familiar with the simple techniques of effective networking, you tend to stick within your comfort zone at these events. It is comfortable to hang out with our friends or to stand in the corner and wait for lunch to begin. Yes, even eating rubber chicken seems to be a better option than talking to a stranger. However, this is not taking advantage of the opportunities at hand. Unless you are making new contacts your network is not growing.

Give Yourself Permission

"You have to give yourself permission to network," was my first comment to the group at the luncheon meeting. Changing your attitude to a positive one is the first step to success. Just allowing yourself that "switch" in your mindset can make all the difference. Then you need some techniques you can use immediately when you walk into that room full of people or when someone announces, "It's time to network!"

Twelve Techniques to Use When "It's Time to Network"

Here are twelve techniques you can use immediately to become an effective networker.

1. Have an opening line

2. Develop a 30-second infomercial about yourself

3. Do your research

4. Have a list of "get to know you" questions

5. Develop a list of idea generator topics (small talk)

6. Get in line

7. Take a deep breath and dive into a group

8. Look for a designated greeter or host

9. Introduce yourself to the speaker

10. Start a conversation with your dinner partner

11. Have an exit strategy

12. Set a goal for every event you attend

#1. Have an Opening Line

Think about what you will say in advance when meeting someone new. Prepare several "opening lines" and try them out on several people you want to meet. The more you use them, the easier they will flow. As with anything you practice, using these "opening lines" will soon become natural. Here are some ideas:

- "I'm thinking of joining this group. Are you a member? How have you found their programs (meetings, get-togethers, resources, etc.)?"
- "What brought you to this meeting?"
- "I'm new here—what can you tell me about this group?"
- "I'm a new member of this group and this is my first meeting (convention, seminar, etc.). How does this compare to others you've attended?"
- "What business are you in? How useful do you find these meetings to be?"
- "Have you heard the speaker before? What do you know about him?"
- "What are some of the benefits of this association?"

Notice that most of these are "open-ended" questions, which require more than a one-word answer. The trick is to get the other person talking and to start a conversation. Then you will have broken the ice!

#2. Develop a 30-Second Infomercial about Yourself

Be prepared to introduce yourself and to answer the question, "What do you do?" in thirty seconds or less—in a clear, concise, enthusiastic, and memorable way. Think of this as your 30-second infomercial. Remember, first impressions count, and you have a limited time to make a good impression.

Answer the following questions when developing your 30-second infomercial:

■ Does the answer to "what do you do?" let the other person know what I want to be known for?

Often it is easiest just to state your title, position, or profession. "I'm an investment

Develop a Sound S.T.R.A.T.E.G.Y. for Your 30-Second Infomercial

S–Make your infomercial <u>S</u>hort and <u>S</u>uccinct.

T–<u>T</u>hink of it in advance.

R–<u>R</u>emember the <u>R</u>esults you wish to achieve.

A–Be <u>A</u>rticulate in your message.

T–<u>T</u>ime is of the essence— 30 seconds is optimal.

E–Speak with <u>E</u>nthusiasm and <u>E</u>nergy.

G–Set a <u>G</u>oal to attain.

Y–Focus on "<u>Y</u>ou" (the other person).

advisor." " I'm vice-president of sales for ABC Tools." " I'm a computer con-sultant." "I'm a marketing manager for XYZ Corporation." "I'm a real estate agent." "I'm a CPA." Or, in my case, I might say, "I run a training and devel-opment company." These answers are all fine if they truly tell your audience who you are. However, consider these instead: "I help people retire (send their kids to college, build their dream house...)", "I coach salespeople on how to exceed their goals", "I make computers friendly" , "I develop win-ning marketing campaigns" , "I find people their dream home" , " I save people money on their taxes." And, in my case, "I create superstars out of executives." A bit corny? Or is it just reflective of who you are and how you want to be known? Memorable? Yes. A conversation starter? Definitely. My doctor's reply to the "what do you do" question is, "I keep people breath-ing." It works for him because this is why he became a doctor and how he wants to be known. Find a line that works for you.

■ Does it make the other person say, "Oh really—how do you do that?"

Whatever your response to "what do you do" or the opening of your 30-second infomercial, make your statement evoke the question, "Oh really—how do you do that?" This starts a conversation and gives you the oppor-tunity to sell yourself based on the interests of the other person. Many times, when I open with "I create superstars out of executives," the response is "How do you do that?" I then respond, "Workshops, seminars, and speaking engagements." Now I can develop and build the conversation depending on the interests of the other person. Often I am asked who attends, or who books these workshops, seminars, and speaking engagements. This gives me an opportunity to describe my target audience. If the person I am speaking with is the target, great. If not, maybe they know someone who is. This is networking!

■ Are you specific enough?

Paint a word picture in the other person's mind. Remember that since we all meet so many people it is important to make ourselves stand out. Otherwise, you will be one in a sea of names that all end up underwater. Give specific examples of who you are, what you do, and who your target audience is so that others will not only remember you, but can comfortably refer you. I have a friend who is so vague and inarticulate that I can't even tell you what it is he does. He is nice enough, and I would be glad to help him out, but I simply don't know how.

■ Are you enthusiastic and upbeat?

Do you enjoy what you do, and does it show? If you are excited about what you do and you have developed the answer to the question, "what do you do?" to reflect this passion, then you will naturally come across as an enthusiastic and upbeat person. I have seen it so many times. No matter what your personality type, you come across as a positive and enthusiastic person.

Enthusiasm is a loaded word. Some people think it means high energy, jumping up and down, and exuberance. I think it means showing a sincere interest in your work, other people, and life in general. Even quiet people can be enthusiastic. In some stressful situations such as having just lost your job, or being in a room full of strangers, you have to consciously work at showing your true enthusiasm. You have to act as if you feel enthusiastic. Do this and you will soon feel enthusiastic. It works!

#3. Do Your Research

Before you attend a meeting or event, research the company or organization putting it on. Research the speaker, the topic, and the issues relevant to the meeting. This is easy enough to do on the Internet. You can type any topic, person, or organization into a search engine and in seconds have more information than you need. To make all this manageable, look first for the most current material. I check the "press room" or "news center" to find the latest information or the latest press release from the company or about the person or industry I am researching. Then I also check through some "history" files to get a feel for the organization, speaker, or topic.

Read either print or electronic versions of industry, association, and trade magazines and newsletters. I find lots of articles and news items about promotions, job changes, and other news events that present opportunities for me to start a conversation with someone. If you spend some time doing research you can also easily develop opening lines based on your new knowledge. The extra time you spend on the Internet will be "net worth" it!

#4. Have A List Of "Get To Know You" Questions

"Get to know you" questions are different from your opening lines in that they focus on the person you are speaking with, not the event or organization.

Here is a story about how "get to know you" questions work. Several years ago I was in London to give a workshop. When I entered the auditorium to set up I found a room full of people all sitting quietly in their seats, staring straight ahead. So I asked them, "Are you all here waiting for my session to begin or are you still spellbound from the one that just ended?" I got a chuckle. It turned out they were waiting for my session which was not scheduled to begin for another twenty minutes. " Great," I said, "Here's your chance to get to know your neighbors." You would have thought I had asked them to give a fifteen-minute presentation in front of the group. No one moved. Finally, one man raised his hand and said, "We don't do that over here." Smiling, I replied, "People don't do that very much where I'm from either yet I've found it is a wonderful way to connect with someone, pass the time, and even learn something new about each other. People love to follow specific instructions, so I asked them to turn to their neighbor and ask the following questions:

- Why did you come to this session?
- Where do you work and what do you do?
- Where do you live?
- What other sessions have you attended?
- What do you do when you are not working?
- What do you love about your work?
- What type of projects do you get involved in and what have you done recently?

At first nothing happened, and then about thirty seconds later they all started talking at once and kept at it. It was hard to get them to stop so I could start the session. When I finally got their attention again, I asked one of my favorite questions, "Who just met someone interesting?" Of course, all hands went up. Then I asked them to share a few things they had learned about each other. People discovered they had friends in common, grew up in the same neighborhoods, and had shared interests and hobbies. More importantly to their business lives, they met colleagues who could help with projects, they learned about parts of the company they had never known about, and they learned how they could become a resource for others.

Develop your own set of personal and business-related "get to know you" questions. You can use the ones above as a guide. Add questions relating to family, travel, hobbies, favorite books and movies, and the like. Add business-related questions appropriate to the situation. Then try them out at your next event. I guarantee you will meet someone interesting.

#5. Develop A List of Idea Generator Topics (Small Talk)

Write ideas down as you think of them. Consider keeping a journal organized by topic. Become conversant about current affairs, best selling books, movies, business news, the stock market, and certainly the latest news and trends in your own industry. Develop opening lines around some of these topics: "What did you think of the State of the Union Address?", "Where were you on September 11?", "What books do you recommend?",

Here's a Quick Tip on Where to Find Idea Generators

Read *The Wall Street Journal* everyday. It is easy to read, it is well written, and it covers a variety of topics, not just finance and business. You will learn a lot. Just a quick read of page one will give you many idea generators.

"What did you think of the Academy Awards?" Occasionally you may find yourself in disagreement with another. Not a problem, just gracefully move on to another topic or another person. The bonus you get for doing your small talk research is, of course, that you become smarter and more well rounded. People love to talk with people who are well rounded and knowledgeable.

#6. Get in Line

Head for the bar, refreshment table, and registration desk—wherever there is a line. When you are standing in a line, there is a natural opportunity to start a conversation with the person in front or back of you. Here is an example of how networking while standing in a line worked for me.

It was 11:30 in the morning, right before lunch, and there was a line in front of the ladies room (where else!) at the hotel where I was attending a meeting. I noticed the nametag on the woman in front of me and realized we were going to the same meeting. "Have you come to these meetings before? What do you think of them?" I asked her. As we chatted I learned she was the vice-president of a cable company. By the time we reached the end of the line, we had exchanged cards with a promise that I would send her some information about my seminars. Seven months later the woman became a client of mine. All because we started talking in line for the ladies' room.

#7. Take a Deep Breath and Dive into a Group

Look for a group that looks friendly, wait for an opening, and say, "I don't mean to interrupt, but you seem like a friendly group. I'm new here. Would you mind if I joined you?" Who could say no to this? Often when I use this approach, people smile and say to me, "You have courage. I admire the fact you can do this. It's nice to meet you."

Once, shortly after I had walked into a meeting where I knew no one, a photographer grabbed me and pushed me into a group to have our picture taken for the group's newsletter. I smiled for the photographer and after he took the picture, I said to the group, "Hi, I'm new here. Are you all members?" After each person introduced himself or herself, I followed using my 30-second infomercial. Then, with some "get to know you questions" the conversation began.

Admittedly, approaching others already in a group is not easy. Even with all of your preparation it can be uncomfortable. So, do what I do sometimes—give yourself a pep talk! Write down a couple of positive and interesting things about yourself, such as:

- I am glad to be here.
- I am a great listener.
- I am a friendly person and eager to learn and meet new people.

■ I am an expert in my field and eager to be a resource to others.

Positive self-talk really does work!

#8. Look for a Designated Greeter or Host and Introduce Yourself

It is part of a host's job to introduce you to others, especially when you are a new member or a visitor thinking of joining the group. Ask the host for help.

One night at an association event cocktail party, I lingered after checking in and reading the nametag on a woman at the registration desk said, "Barbara, it is nice to meet you. I've read your organization's newsletter and it sounds like you have a lot of active members. Could I ask your help in introducing me to a couple of people here to break the ice?" She gladly took me around to several people with whom I was able to talk for the remainder of the evening. When I came to the next meeting, I was more comfortable and walked right over to reconnect with those I had met earlier. Of course, I followed up with a short note to thank Barbara for introducing me around. (There is more on the importance of thank-you notes in Chapter 7.)

#9. Introduce Yourself to the Speaker

Tell him or her how much you are looking forward to the talk and mention something specific about the topic or speaker. Of course, you will have done your research ahead of time and will know these tidbits. Remember to check out the speaker's website for information, a bio, or a book. After the presentation follow up by sending a note saying how much you enjoyed the talk and mentioning a helpful piece of information you took away. Remind the speaker in the note that you spoke together beforehand. He or she will remember you.

Several months ago at a conference, I had the opportunity to chat with the luncheon keynote speaker before the program. I had done my homework and knew she was responsible for a recent new product launch. She was impressed I had read the press release on the company website, especially since it had just been posted that week. The speaker also was the executive director of a well-known association I had been hoping to join. When I mentioned this, she asked that I follow up with her. Of course I did and I am now a member of that organization.

You need to be careful when approaching speakers before their program. Be sensitive to their body language. Some speakers are a bit nervous before a presentation. Some may be "rehearsing" their talk in their mind and may not be receptive to your approach. If you sense this, just tell them you are looking forward to hearing their presentation and move on.

#10. Start a Conversation with Your Dinner Partner

At a seated meal, the person on your right or left is the logical person to engage. Use your opening lines and your idea generators and start the con-

Sometimes It's Perfectly Fine to Seek Out People You Already Know at a Networking Event

While the main purpose of a networking event is to meet and connect with new people, staying in touch and nurturing relationships with those you already know is also effective networking. Often, a long-overdue reunion with an old friend can be "net-worthwhile." That was the case at a recent event where I spotted my friend Roz.

Roz and I had met previously through a mutual contact and had subsequently met for coffee and stayed in touch via phone calls. While attending an association meeting of a group I had just joined I saw she was

versation rolling. Otherwise, you will be paying too much good attention to a bad meal. After all, these meals are not about the food, they are about connecting and learning from others.

#11. Have an Exit Strategy

Even when we're engrossed in a great conversation with someone it is perfectly polite to leave something for next time and close your conversation with a follow-up plan in order to move on and talk with someone else. The other scenario that calls for an exit strategy is when you are talking with someone and you find yourself mentally counting the minutes to get away. Whatever the situation, here are some exit lines to practice:

- "It was great meeting you and hopefully we can continue our conversation sometime over lunch or coffee."
- "Thanks for sharing the information about your new project. It sounds exciting. Best of continued success."

- "Please excuse me, I see a friend that I'd like to go over and visit with."
- "I enjoyed hearing about your company. I'll see you again. Enjoy the rest of the evening."
- "You've been so interesting to talk with. I'll let you have the opportunity to share your thoughts with some other folks."

#12. Set a Goal for Every Event You Attend

Carl, one of my clients, used to stand in a corner at company meetings and other gatherings while folks around him were meeting and having conversations. Although he is a highly respected executive, he suffered from severe shyness (familiar to many of us) that made him very uncomfortable in networking situations. Often, he would attend these meetings with his associate, Jerry, who was extremely gregarious and social. Carl knew he had to make business contacts and he also desperately wanted to

there and I immediately started a conversation with her. I discovered she was a regular member of this association. I not only found out a lot about the association through our conversation, but I also found out more about her and her organization. As a follow-up, we met for lunch, and over the next few months we met several other times to discuss working together on some projects.

Three months later, Roz took on an extensive consulting project for a client and brought me in to work with them on team building. You never know when and how opportunities develop. Just set the process in motion, keep in contact, and be patient.

have more interactions. Attending these events with Jerry put added pressure on Carl because he thought he could not keep up with Jerry.

"Begin slowly," I told him. "Set a goal before you leave the office to meet two new people. This does not mean you cannot meet more than two. However, your goal is to meet just two new people with whom you will engage in conversation, ask some open-ended questions, and exchange pleasantries." I also told him that if he felt there was a reason to meet again, he should send a note, e-mail, or call to set up a follow-up meeting over breakfast or lunch. In any event, he should send a short "thank you for your time and conversation" to the two people he met even if there was no future meeting. I told him this was just common courtesy and would serve him well as a respected leader.

The key for Carl, and for you, is to set a goal to make a set number of quality connections (Carl's was two) at every meeting, gathering, or event you attend, and then make yourself go through the process. Also, be sure to follow up.

These twelve techniques will help you get through any networking event with confidence. Once you start practicing and applying them, you will find yourself actually looking forward to networking events as you continue to expand your network and enrich your life.

Eight Essential Communication Skills

Armed with these techniques, the next step is to master some communication fundamentals in order to keep your network alive and growing. The best communicators know how to:

1. **Smile**

2. **Look the person in the eye**

3. **Listen**

4. **Remember names**

5. **Be aware of body language**

6. **Be respectful of other's boundaries**

7. **Look for common interests**

8. **Give genuine compliments**

#1. Smile

A smile is the first step in building rapport. Remember to smile when you enter a room, a business meeting, and even when you answer the phone. I give people mirrors with the phrase printed on the case, "Can your smile be heard?" I tell them to put the mirror on their desk when they are talking on the phone in order to see their expression. And, yes, a smile can be heard. Remember also, when you are talking with someone face-to-face,

The Good, the Bad, and the Ugly about Nametags

Nametags are very helpful at networking events such as trade shows, where often a person's company and type of business are displayed along with his or her name. However, some people violate common courtesy when using them. My friend Judy tells me the story of attending a trade show with Stephen, a consultant to her business. "We entered a booth and were approached by the owner, who smiled and held out her hand in greeting. However, upon glancing at Stephen's nametag, which was color-coded as a business con-

that person becomes the mirror that reflects your expression. Your expression is the most important thing you wear. Smiling can raise your spirits and can even affect the way you sound. A smile can also disarm another. Use this powerful communication tool to your advantage.

#2. Look the Other Person in the Eye

Making good eye contact shows respect and interest. Have you ever been speaking with a person who was looking over your shoulder instead of at you? Did you feel like, "He doesn't think I'm important." Or, "He's not even listening to me?"

Once at a trade show I was talking to a man who spent the whole five minutes of a conversation that he had initiated looking everywhere except at me. In fact, at one point he saw someone he obviously wanted to speak with and in mid-sentence, he turned around and began speaking with the other person as if I had evaporated into thin air.

Eye contact is one of the strongest communication skills we can develop. It's been said, and I believe it is true, "The eyes are the windows of the soul."

#3. Listen With Care

One of the greatest compliments you can give another is to let him or her know you are listening to everything said. Find the hidden word in LISTEN using all the letters. The word is SILENT. That is what our internal voice must be to get the full impact of what others are saying. Remember that when you are networking with a new contact, it is like reading the paper. Let the person tell you the story so you can discover the "news you can use." More people have literally talked themselves out of a job or a sale by talking instead of sitting back and actively listening. It takes real concentration to listen.

sultant to the industry, she obviously decided we would be of no use to her. Her smile faded, her hand receded, and she walked right past us in search of more promising contacts. She must have thought Stephen was there to sell her something when in fact he was working for my company, which could have become her company's customer. She made a snap judgment based on the nametag, and worse yet, she was extremely rude to both of us. She is off my list of prospective contacts—that is for sure." Two points to this story: Do not make snap judgments about people, and above all, remember your manners.

Are You a Good Listener?

Rate yourself on how consistently you use these ten listening skills on a scale of 1-5 with 1 being "I consistently use this skill" and 5 being "do not use this skill consistently."

1. I make eye contact.
2. I ask questions for clarification.
3. I show concern by acknowledging feelings.
4. I restate or paraphrase to show I understand.
5. I try to understand the speaker's point of view before giving mine.
6. I am poised and emotionally controlled.
7. I react non-verbally with a smile or a nod.
8. I pay close attention and do not let my mind wander.
9. I am responsible for what I hear.
10. I don't change the subject without warning.

Look at the areas where you rated yourself three or higher. Start to work on these, while continuing to practice the skills you do consistently. Take the test again in two weeks. Your ratings will change positively when you commit to improving your listening skills.

#4. Remember Names

Dale Carnegie, author of *How to Win Friends and Influence People* says, "...a person's name is to him or her the sweetest and most important sound in any language."

It pays to remember names. Here are three ways to sharpen your name remembering skills.

1. Form an impression of the person's appearance and embed it into your mind. Note height, stature, color of hair and eyes, facial expression, and any distinguishing physical features. Do not concentrate so much on dress, or even hairstyle. These may be different the next time you meet.

2. Repeat the person's name after you meet and several times during the conversation. When you repeat the name two things happen—the person is flattered and the name goes into your memory bank.

3. Make up a visual story about the person's name. Associate the person's name with something that will remind you of it. Use your imagination and build a mind picture. Put the person into your visual story. The sillier the story, the easier it will be to remember. Here is an example of how to remember my name with a visual story.

My name is Andrea Nierenberg. Picture me in the Antarctic, dressed in white fur, clinging to the bow of a sinking ship, the "Andrea Doria" (Andrea) which is "near an iceberg" (Nier-en-berg). There you have a picture of me and my name, Andrea Nierenberg. Remember, the sillier the visual story, the easier it is to remember.

#5. Be Aware of Your Body Language

"What you do speaks so loudly that I cannot hear what you say."—Ralph Waldo Emerson.

You can say a lot without ever opening your mouth. Research tells us perceptions are formed in three ways: Verbal makes up 7 percent, non-verbal 38 percent, and visual is 55 percent of our perception of others. Notice that body language makes up the biggest percentage. Make sure your body language communicates what you truly want to say.

B–Breathe deeply and consistently. This steadies your nerves and gives you a pleasant facial expression that says, "I'm glad to be speaking with you."

O–Overtures can speak volumes. Nod to show encouragement and to show you are listening. Keep an open posture to show you are receptive.

D–Demeanor is the part of your personality demonstrated by body language. A blank stare, crossed arms, nervous gestures, all convey the opposite of what you want to communicate.

Y–"You," meaning the other person, should be your main focus. Observe how others interact and find a way to match it. For example, if you are sitting across the table from a person who is leaning in to create a closer connection, follow suit. Do not lean back; this says, "I'm not interested."

#6. Be Respectful of Other's Boundaries

The invisible boundaries around us define our personal space. These vary from culture to culture. Most Americans become uncomfortable if someone is closer than eighteen inches. In some countries, standing as close as we do in the United States is considered too far apart. In other places, it is too close. People's boundaries are not only an issue for travelers. America is a melting pot so you need to be aware of the diversity within our own country.

#7. Look for Common Interests

Ask open-ended questions and then listen to what others have to say. Develop your list of "get to know you questions" so they are easy and automatic. Make sure they are phrased so that they cannot be answered with just one word. Or at least have a follow-up question ready. Some people you meet—you probably know the type—will take your questions quite literally. "Did you enjoy the speaker?" you ask, hoping to start a conversation. "Yes" is the answer you get, followed by silence. So change your question to, "How did you find the speaker's presentation?" You may still get, "Fine." But then you can follow up with, "What did you particularly like about it?"

Once you establish your common interests, the conversation will flow, and you will easily find reasons to follow up and keep in touch.

#8. Give Genuine Compliments

When you listen to someone carefully, often they will mention something about which they are proud. Think for a moment and find a way to acknowledge the person's achievement.

"Five-a-Day"

Look for positive attributes in the people you come in contact with during the course of your day, and compliment them. Make a goal to give "five-a-day." Put five pennies in your left-hand pocket at the beginning of a day. Each time you give a sincere compliment, take a penny and put it into your right-hand pocket. By the end of the day, you should have transferred all five pennies to make the goal. Try it and see how you do!

Make a goal of finding at least one positive trait or characteristic in each person you meet that you can compliment. It may seem awkward at first, but soon it will become second nature.

As a general rule, most of us do not give out compliments as often as they might be deserved. We worry that we will come across as phony or as if we are doing it because we want something. This is why it is so critical to be sincere and to give a compliment only when you mean it.

Sometimes you may give someone a compliment and the recipient will not know how to receive it. It is a common reaction. Do not let this stop you from giving compliments. Everybody likes to be complimented, even if they do not know how to show it.

In Summary

This chapter has described the importance of giving yourself permission to network, the twelve techniques for successful networking, and finally, the eight essential skills you need to become a better communicator. Be confident that these techniques and communication fundamentals will work over time when practiced conscientiously. Use them with anyone—your boss, a business colleague, a neighbor, or a family member. These are all people you need in your network, as you will discover in the next chapter.

Chapter 3

People You Need In Your Network

Networking is not just for networking events or for when we are told, "It's time to network." Networking is a way of life. We do it all the time without even realizing it. In this chapter I will help you identify the types of people you will want to include in your network. You will discover that many of them are already in your life. "I don't have time to network. I'm already too busy to be with my friends and to do the things I want to do!" Does this sound familiar? Would you like to know how these people and activities fit right into your busy life and can be part of your networking success story?

It's a Small World

The truth is, almost everybody with whom you come into contact—a prospect, client, friend, family member—either is or knows someone from whom you can learn something that could

This Book Came About Through "Six Degrees of Separation"

My publicist, Tom (the first person in the path) introduced me to an editor, Florence (the second person). She, in turn introduced me to another editor at her firm, Susan (the third person), who was looking for an authority on self-marketing to endorse a book on the subject. That book—which I read and endorsed—went to Elizabeth, a literary agent (the fourth person), who sent it to Judy (the fifth person), an acquisitions editor at Capital Books. Judy remembered me from our working together several years back. When she saw my endorsement she posed the idea of writing a book about networking to me. I agreed and sent a proposal, which she presented to Capital Book's publisher, Kathleen (the sixth and last person in the path), who published the

benefit your business, profession, personal life, or even your hobbies and interests. There is a name for this phenomenon. It is the "small world effect" and it is based on the notion that through just five or six intermediaries you could be linked to literally millions of others in this world. Another way of stating this is that everyone in the world is connected to everyone else through a path of six people or fewer. You may have heard this called "six degrees of separation." Based on this theory, almost anyone you meet is potentially of help to you.

You can see the small world phenomenon all around you. Often there are even fewer than six degrees of separation between you and a decision-maker. While shopping at Bloomingdales in New York recently, I asked one of the cosmetic managers if she knew Robin, a brand manager with whom I had worked on a project. She did and was delighted to tell me that Robin had been promoted. I immediately sent Robin a note of congratulations.

Later we met for lunch, where she introduced me to her new boss who told me about an upcoming project I might manage. Her boss in turn introduced me to the decision-maker for the project and I got the job. It is a small world. Yet keep in mind, connections happen only when you work on establishing and maintaining relationships.

Types of People

An important first step is to identify the people with whom you want to build relationships. The types of people you need in your network include:

1. **Customers or clients**

2. **Suppliers**

3. **Neighbors**

4. **Like-minded people**

5. **People you meet by chance**

6. **Friends**

7. **Family**

book you are now reading. These events did not happen overnight, nor were they planned. The relationships in this path developed over time. Tom and I have worked together for six years, I've known Florence for five years, and Judy and I first met over fifteen years ago. Who knew then how these relationships would lead ultimately to Kathleen, who would publish this book!

Who Would Return Your Phone Call?

Write down the names of people you know in each of the seven categories. Don't think about how they might be able to help you. Just write down the names for now. You may have collected lots of names and business cards through the years. Write down only the names of people who would take your phone call or return your phone call. This is your network.

You Already Have a Much Larger Network Than You Think

How many people do you work with?

How many people have you worked with in the past?

How many clients do you have?

How many people do you know from professional organizations?

How many people do you know from other organizations such as health clubs, your homeowners association, or PTA?

How many people do you know from religious affiliations or organizations?

How many professionals (doctors, lawyers, and accountants) do you deal with?

How many former schoolmates do you stay in touch with?

How many people do you know in your neighborhood?

How many friends and relatives do you have?

#1. Customers or Clients

These people are your business lifeblood and it is important to build positive relationships with them. The more you know about them and the more they know about and trust you, the more both of you will prosper.

You might be thinking, "This category does not apply to me. I don't have customers or clients." In my seminars, I often ask, "By a show of hands, how many of you are in sales? How many in customer service? How many are in public relations? How many own and run a business?" Some hands go up. Then I ask, "How many of you have to convince another person to use an idea of yours? How many of you are looking for a new job, a promotion, a raise?" By the end of my questions, almost everyone has raised their hand. The reality is that we are all in sales, customer service, or public relations whatever our business position is.

If you think about it, you are constantly communicating messages and selling your ideas to others. We are all public relations managers when we act as a representative of our company or of ourselves. Your clients include co-workers, staff, other department heads, and certainly your boss. In fact, anyone you sell your thoughts or ideas to is a client—even people in your neighborhood association, church group, or PTA.

If you are in sales—and we all are—loyal, happy customers can be profitable members of your network. They can refer you to prospects and thereby help you grow your network. Here are some networking tactics to keep your customers satisfied:

- Know your customers. Find out hobbies, names of family members, likes and dislikes, and birthdays. Keep good records on this information and use it to build on your relationships. (More on this in chapter 9.)

- Keep in touch. Share information and ideas with customers when you believe it will help them. Even if nothing happens, it will provide an opportunity to stay in touch. Remember, your goal is to build a relationship.

- Handle complaints promptly. Take responsibility for problems no matter who or what was the cause. Your customers will see you as their helper and help you in return.

■ Prove that you are dependable. When you make promises keep them! This builds trust, an important factor in any relationship.

#2. Suppliers

Whether you own a business or not, you buy goods and services from suppliers. Think of all the products and services you buy—not just for business but also for personal use.

Besides business contacts, your suppliers might include your dry cleaner, your hairdresser, and yes, even your dentist! My dentist, Alan, is a valued member of my network. I have recommended him to friends, and he tells his patients about my services. On one occasion, he even dragged me out of the dental chair, my mouth numb from a novocain injection, to introduce me to the woman in the next chair. With her mouth filled with cotton swabs, she, too, could not speak. So he proceeded to explain to her why she needed someone with my talents. We exchanged business cards, I followed up, and in time, she became a client of mine.

#3. Neighbors

Neighbors can serendipitously become valuable members of your network. Many of us do not know our neighbors very well. Often we just wave "hi" as they drive by or we chat about our gardens, traffic, or the weather. Sometimes we even avoid eye contact in our building elevator.

Get to know your neighbors by using some of the networking techniques from Chapter 2. Try some of your opening lines, conversation starters, and your 30-second infomercial. You might be surprised to find a neighbor who is in the same business, or a related business, or who knows someone you want to meet (small world, again). Of course, good neighbors are always an invaluable source for such things as cleaning services, yard people, painters, electricians, plumbers, decorators, and when the time comes to move away—realtors. I'm sure many of you are well aware of this and are networking in your neighborhood. You may not call this "networking"—yet it is and you are already very good at it.

#4. Like-Minded People

I don't know about you, but I find the easiest people to talk to are people who share my interests, have similar ambitions, or who have

Why You Should Network in Your Elevator

One morning as I was in the elevator of my apartment building, a neighbor stepped in carrying an obviously expensive laptop computer. We exchanged pleasantries and then I said, "Excuse me, I couldn't help noticing your nice laptop. Would you happen to know of a good computer consultant?" He replied, "I'm a computer consultant." Because of our elevator conversation, we formed a mutually beneficial business relationship. He was my computer consultant for many years and, as he became familiar with my work, he referred me to many of his clients who became clients of mine, or who introduced me to other prospects.

There seems to be a convention about not talking to people in elevators. I personally have found that networking can take place anywhere—even in an elevator!

Networking Can Happen Anywhere

As I was getting my nails done one morning, I started a conversation with the woman next to me. I noticed she had a deep tan and as I had just done a workshop at a conference for tanning salon owners, I used my newly found knowledge about tanning as a conversation starter. I asked her where she got her tan and then we started a dialogue about the reason I had been at the tanning salon owners' convention. I gave her my 30-second infomercial. With wet fingernails, we exchanged business cards and I later followed up, sending her materials about my services. She is a partner at a major law firm and I have subsequently done several projects for her firm.

had similar life experiences. Where do you find these like-minded people? Obvious places are in business meetings, at conferences, association meetings, trade shows, or wherever folks in your industry gather formally or informally to share ideas or to learn new skills and news about your industry. These people share an interest in your profession. It is an obvious and profitable networking strategy to seek out these places and these people. When you want to be successful in your profession, you will join trade associations, interest groups, attend seminars, workshops, and conventions, and become an active participant in these gatherings.

"But wait," you say. "I have a life! What about my photography class, writing seminars, PTA meetings, my kid's soccer games and recitals, trips to the museum, my weekend at the spa—the stuff I really like to do!" Well, actually, the people you find at these events like the same things you do. That is why they are there—which leads to a perfect networking opportunity.

Six years ago, I attended a Saturday morning workshop about Creative Visualization. "What does this have to do with your business, Andrea?" you say. Nothing directly, I was just interested in the topic. The woman seated next to me was a magazine editor who was also there because the topic interested her. Elaine and I met at a break and later became so engrossed in conversation over lunch that we almost forgot to get back to the class. Over the years, Elaine has become a good friend, a client, and a continual source of business support and referrals. She would say the same of me. It all started because we took a class in a subject of interest to us both.

#5. People You Meet by Chance

This is where the fun starts! These networking opportunities sometimes just happen. The fact is, you can meet people and network almost any-where—on the street, in an airplane, in a deli, or even in the ladies room! (Remember the story about the line to the ladies' room from Chapter 2?)

On the street one evening as I was running to meet a friend for dinner I heard someone call out my name. It was Gary, who had worked at the same company I did fifteen years ago. He endeared himself to me imme-diately with wonderful flattery. "You look just like you did when we worked together," he said. He is now a florist. I'm always sending flowers—so guess who became my new florist?

Another chance meeting occurred on a trip back to New York from Dallas after delivering a seminar. Because of an upgrade, I was happily sitting in first class and looking forward to peace and quiet while I wrote follow-up notes to people from my seminar. I pulled out my note cards (more about these in Chapter 7), began to write, and kept writing the whole trip. The man sitting next to me said nothing until we started to land in New York. Then he said, "Excuse me. Are you a professional note writer?" I laughed and explained that I was following up from a sales class I had just given and wanted to get my thank-you notes written while things were fresh in my mind. We introduced ourselves and I found out he was the chairman of a mid-size securities firm. After we chatted a bit, he said, "Can you teach my sales force how to follow up with their customers as well as you are doing?" Of course I could. He is now a client. (By the way, you can write thirty-six thank-you notes between Dallas and New York City.)

#6. Personal Friends

Friends make the world a happier place. We need to welcome and to nurture these people in our lives. By all means, make time for your friends. Never sacrifice friendship for business. No tombstone that I know of says, "He leaves behind many beloved business associates." Take time to nurture and cultivate your friends. And network with them in a positive way—without expectations. Give without the thought of receiving and you will receive the greatest gift of all—a good friend. If something more comes of it, consider it a gift.

My dear friend Lois an author, speaker, and owner of an advertising agency, is at the top of my "A" networking list (more on my list categories in Chapter 7). Several years ago while we both were attending an industry conference, I met a man who was looking for speakers for a project in Sweden. He had already hired me as a speaker for his project, so when we met in San Francisco, I told him about Lois and invited him to attend her workshop. He enjoyed it and seemed interested in hiring her. However, she had to dash off to another workshop and could not speak with him. Therefore, I closed the deal with him and got her the job. We went to Sweden together. It was a great trip and both our presentations were successful. The best part was how good it felt to help a friend who deserved it. And, believe me, over the years she has more than returned the favor to me.

How do you find the time to see your friends? Make plans to meet for breakfast, lunch, or dinner. Even better, look for unusual activities to share. I have met friends for manicures, for "high tea" at three in the afternoon, for shopping excursions, for work outs at the gym (you can definitely chat on the treadmill or bike—it is also good for your heart!), for walks or runs.

Go to a sports event, play golf (the ultimate networking activity), or have a beer after work.

Something to keep in mind is that the "I" in networking stands for Integrity. You may love your friends, just make sure they represent you well if you are going to recommend them, as you would with any recommendation.

#7. Family

Network with the family? Why not? A friend of mine recently told me she recommended her nephew, a graphic artist, for a project for her company. She was familiar with his work and was confident he could do a quality job, quote a reasonable price, and meet the deadlines. Otherwise, she would not have made the recommendation. Remember that her reputation was at stake as it would have been with any recommendation she made. She also wisely distanced herself from the financial negotiations. Both she and her nephew were very clear with each other that this was a business arrangement and no matter the outcome, it would remain so. In this case, it worked out just fine. He did a good job, as she knew he would, and has received several subsequent assignments.

My cousin Hannah opened the door for me into a large organization where she is a senior lawyer. She made the introduction and then she said,

"You're on your own." I continually thank her because I've gone on to do a lot of work with her firm. As she reminds me, she merely opened the door. I kept it open!

Networking with your family can work. Just make sure to maintain your integrity and be mindful of reputations involved.

These are the types of people that should be in your network. Notice the list includes just about everyone in your life, even those you meet by chance. This is a key element of your nonstop networking effort: Opportunities are all around you; you just have to be aware of them and then take advantage of them.

It's Easy to Network with These People

Would you agree that certain people are easier to network with than others are? In this next section, I'll point out some of the characteristics to look for in people that will make building connections easy and beneficial. The people with whom you want to develop mutually beneficial relationships are:

- Happy, helpful people

- Active, involved people

- Ambitious people

- Caring people

Happy, Helpful People

When they see an opportunity to help others, these folks grab it. They just seem to enjoy life. Upbeat and happy, they like to pass these good feelings on to others. Here's an example of how such a person reached out to me. Teresa, a friendly checkout clerk at my mother's grocery store in Florida, introduced herself as she packed our purchases. I noticed her tag signified she was also in the training department so I inquired if the store did outside training programs. Without hesitation, she invited me to observe a training session the next day, where she greeted me enthusiastically and introduced me to her manager, a decision-maker for purchasing training programs. Although nothing has materialized yet from this meeting, Teresa and I are still in contact and I stop by to say "hi" whenever I'm in Florida. She was very helpful to me and is someone I want in my network.

Active, Involved People

"If you want something done, ask a busy person." This is as applicable in networking as it is in the working world. No matter how many contacts they have, or how busy these people are, they are always willing to meet and to help others.

On a long cross-country flight last fall, I fell into conversation with Ben, a lawyer. He told me how volunteering to chair an association event changed his business life. This project took a lot of his time, most of it spent in the company of another volunteer. As it turns out, this volunteer had recently been named president of a large investment bank. As the two worked together they got to know each other, and because the project was long and involved, they formed a solid working relationship. Who do you think the new president handpicked to run a new division of his firm? It was Ben. This connection did not just happen because these two met each other at a meeting. It happened because both were active and involved people.

Ambitious People

These are the go-getters, the people who make things happen. When they tell you they will do something for you, they will. My friend Jeri falls into this category. She is always taking on challenges and projects and she seems to know people who can get things done. She knows them because she is one of them. The advantages in networking with someone like Jeri are twofold. First, when I am around someone like Jeri, I tend to up my own level of ambition. She is a role model. Second, because people like Jeri know so many others, I can expand my network by just staying in touch with her. So, look for common interests and stay in contact with ambitious people.

Caring People

"Who cares, wins!" is the mission statement for a company I once worked for in Hong Kong. The statement is correct. Those who care to go the extra mile for others do win. It helps a business to have people who care on their payroll and it helps you to include them in your network. In addition, it helps you to be a caring person yourself. One of my favorite sayings is, "No one cares how much you know until they know how much you care."

Keep these four traits in mind as you network. People with these characteristics make networking easy and fun. And consider yourself. Are you happy and helpful, active and involved, ambitious, and caring? Do people find you easy to meet and to build a relationship with? Think about how you can develop these characteristics in yourself as well as looking for them in others.

Your List

Now that you are familiar with the categories of people you need in your network, take a look at your own network. Make a list all the people you know by category. Don't think about how they might help you, or even if you want them in your network. For now, just use these simple criteria: If I called this person today, would he or she take my phone call, or at least call me back?

Look in all the places—including in your head and on various yellow stickies—where you have names stored. Look in your address book, Rolodex, business card file, birthday list, computer database of clients, e-mail address book, company directory (current and past), college directory, membership rosters from professional organizations, list of attendees at seminars and workshops you've attended, homeowners association directory, church directory, and others. Use a yellow highlighter to mark the names of folks who would take your call. If you cannot make a list, at least gather all your cards, directories, and phone books in one place—in a file box, even a shoebox. The idea is just to get them all together.

This exercise serves two purposes. First and most importantly, it shows you how many people you already know and how broad your network is. You may never have thought to include people from some of these categories, yet they are useful members of your network. Secondly, it is the first step to organizing your contact list, which we will deal with in more detail in Chapter 9. For now, it should feel good just to gather these names in one place and to know how many resources you now have at your fingertips.

In Summary

Now that you know the type of people you need in your network and characteristics to look for in developing your network, in the next chapter, I will turn the focus back on you. We will take a look at the personal traits of great networkers and how you can develop these traits.

Chapter 4

Characteristics of Great Networkers

Is there someone you know who can walk into a room full of strangers and immediately make friends? Can you recall someone who instantly made you feel at ease when you first met him or her? How about a person who makes you feel as though you are the only person in the world when they are speaking with you?

If you know such a person, or people, take a moment to think about what personal traits they possess. Are they confident? Empathetic? Enthusiastic and energetic? Tenacious? Caring? Appreciative? Chances are they are all of these. How would you like to possess these characteristics as well? Well, you can, and this chapter focuses on how.

Here we will look at each characteristic and discuss how it works in effective networking. As with everything I present, my advice to you is to adapt it to your own personality, lifestyle, and goals as you develop your networking skills.

Effective networkers are:

- **Confident**
- **Empathetic**
- **Appreciative**
- **Tenacious**
- **Enthusiastic and Energetic**
- **Caring**

Confident

Neil is the president of a runner's club that meets for runs on Saturday mornings. He exudes confidence. It shows in the simplest of matters, like how he is able to silence fifty eager runners in order to make announcements before a run, and in far more important matters, such as how he is able to muster an army of volunteers to raise thousands of dollars at a run to benefit cancer research. His confidence is a magnet. People gravitate to him and eagerly offer their time and expertise. Where did Neil's confidence come from? You can't buy it. If there were a store that sold it, we would all be in line. Confidence comes with experience and grows over time. What kind of experience helps us develop it? Not sitting still, not doing the same thing repeatedly and expecting different results. To build confidence you have to step out of your comfort zone and take some risks. It helps if you start with small steps and then keep going as your confidence grows.

Remember Carl from Chapter 2? He had to step out of his comfort zone to meet and follow up with the two people he wanted to connect with at every networking event he attended. He took it in small steps: he made a plan, thought about conversation starters, and followed up. He may have been less than comfortable at first, but the more he did it, the better he became. Soon he was confident in his ability to meet and talk to people, and people were eager to meet him. His confidence made him more relaxed and approachable.

Compare this process to any new thing you have mastered—learning to play tennis, learning to use a computer, speaking in front of a group. You started with small steps and progressed as your competence and confidence grew. Most importantly, you had to step out of

Reach Higher

In my seminars, I ask everyone to stand and raise their hands as high as they can raise them. Then, when they are as high as they can go, I say, "Now, go an inch higher!" Everyone does it. The point is, we can always do better than our best. So keep reaching even higher as you develop your confidence.

To Grow Your Confidence, Start with "Baby Steps"

Taking a ride one lovely Thanksgiving holiday in Cape Cod, I never imagined I would wake up hours later in a hospital emergency room in Boston with thirty-seven broken bones. During my recovery, I had a lot of time to reflect. This terrible automobile accident had shattered more than my bones. I thought I was a confident person, but it all seemed to disappear as I embarked on my journey to recovery.

For starters, I had to learn to walk again. I literally started with "baby steps." With each small step I took, my confidence grew. One day in the hospital, I was able to walk across the room using only a walker to push me along. Granted, it took forty-five minutes, but it was a major accomplishment for me. The doctors and nurses were so proud of me, and I had gained back a bit of my lost confidence.

Confidence grows in small increments: inch-by-inch, it is a cinch; yard-by-yard, it can be hard!

your comfort zone, take a risk, do something different, and then as you continued to practice and got better at the skill, you gained confidence. Did you also notice that people were more interested in what you had to say than before? It was suddenly easier to expand your contacts in your new field of expertise.

To develop confidence, practice the skills you wish to attain. Over time, the confidence you have developed in your abilities will show. As with Neil and Carl, people will be drawn to you because you are a confident person.

Empathetic

An empathetic person puts himself or herself in another's shoes. Being empathetic does not necessarily mean you share another's point of view; it does mean you are concerned about others and are interested in their point of view.

Empathetic people pay attention to the details. They take the time to look and listen to others. They observe and interpret body language. They listen as carefully to what people leave unsaid as to what they say. They have the ability to read between the lines. They can tell when a friend is preoccupied and they respect these boundaries. They have the ability to make the other person truly feel they are heard and valued.

One afternoon as I was working on a speech, I received a call from a business colleague, Susan. Although she tried to sound upbeat, I could tell something was not quite right. Her voice sounded spacey and disconnected. I respected her nonverbal but obvious wish not to discuss what was bothering her over the phone, so I suggested we meet for coffee the next morning. It turned out she had just lost her job and was in a state of shock. Her dismissal had clearly come out of left field. Only the week before, her work had been highly commended.

I listened, observed her body language, made a few comments, and encouraged her as

Seven Traits of Great Networkers

1. Appear confident and are not afraid to ask for what they need

2. Appreciate those who help them

3. Consistently nurture their relationships

4. Are tenacious in going around obstacles

5. Are excellent listeners

6. Rebound quickly and completely from rejection

7. Are friendly and approachable

she began to develop a plan. Even though I did not directly offer advice, she told me later that I had helped her a great deal. A week later, I received a call from a contact at a company who was looking for someone with Susan's skills. I made some calls, meetings were set up, and soon Susan had a new job. I like to think that being empathetic to Susan helped this process. I understood how she felt and what she wanted to do. Then, because both of us are good networkers, she was able to take advantage of an opportunity when it presented itself.

Become Aware of Communication Styles

Empathetic people are aware of communication styles and will accommodate their style to others when appropriate.

We all use different styles of communication when giving and receiving information. Some people are auditory—they learn by hearing information. They can understand a lecture without taking notes. They prefer a verbal briefing to a written report. They like to listen to the news rather than read a newspaper. When speaking with an auditory type, I will be sure to use phrases such as "are we in harmony?" or "How does this sound to you?"

Others are visual—they need to see pictures or "to see in it writing." These are the folks who take lots of notes in lectures and treasure the handouts. They love visuals, PowerPoint presentations, and flip charts. When they communicate, they often draw what they are talking about on a pad. Phrases to use with them might include, "How does this look to you?" or "Picture this...."

Still others are kinesthetic. They need to act things out or have things demonstrated to them. These are people who talk with their hands or who explain how to do something with a demonstration. They learn things best by actually doing them. With these people I have said, "Are you comfortable with this idea?" or "How does this feel to you?"

Think about how you like to give and get information. What is your favored communication style? What is that of your boss, various co-workers, your subordinates, even your spouse? Have you ever been frustrated trying to communicate something when the other person just did not get it? Maybe your communication styles were too disparate. Think about how you could adapt your style to accommodate theirs. Keep in mind, people will not tell

Each communication style has its own language

Visual	Auditory	Kinesthetic
See	Hear	Feel
Look	Listen	Touch
Picture	Sound	Feeling
Appear	Discuss	Aware

you their style. You will pick it up only by observation and careful listening. Hear the words they use and watch their behavior. Then you can match your words to theirs in order to communicate with them effectively.

Being a good listener and an effective communicator are keys to showing empathy. When you hear someone say, "This doesn't sound right to me." An empathetic response is, "What exactly are you hearing to make you say that?"

Adjusting to the Personality Styles of Others

In addition to being aware of communication styles, empathy requires adjusting ourselves to other people's orientation. Some people are more oriented, or sensitive, to the concerns and feeling of others; other people are more "bottom line" or results oriented; and still others are interested and concerned with details and the way things work. This is a simplification of the complex concept of personality styles or behavior types. Study these if you are interested. However, to be empathetic all you really need to do is listen carefully and respect the other person's orientation.

I recently found myself presenting a business proposal to three different decision-makers in an organization. I knew from previous conversations that they had very different personality styles. I needed to show empathy and adjust my presentation to each one individually.

The human resources director was harmonious and amiable in her approach. What I remembered most about her was her comment to me about being sure to "get everyone involved, caring and concern for everyone, and to emphasize the human element." Clearly, I had to focus my presentation to her on the personal benefits for her employees.

The chief financial officer, on the other hand, was interested in the return on investment he would get from my program. He also wanted lots of details. I would give him the same proposal that I had given to the human resources director but much more detailed with a specific outline for each module and with costs clearly defined. The more data I presented, the better.

The CEO would give me only five minutes of his time. And all he wanted to know was, "What are my people going to learn?" and "How much will it cost?" I was prepared with the same presentation (in case he had questions), but gave him only the executive summary: a short, succinct paragraph followed by bullet points and "the bottom line."

These were three very different people—all wanting the same thing yet delivered in three very different ways. In order to succeed, I had to read each person carefully and give him or her back exactly what he or she wanted to hear.

Later, after I had done several programs with the company, each person told me separately how much they liked working with me because, "we communicate in exactly the same way."

An empathetic person is an excellent listener who understands and adapts to the needs of others.

My "Thank-You Chain" Strategy

I am so dedicated to showing appreciation that I created a technique called the "thank-you chain." Here is how it works. After each workshop I conduct, I send a thank-you note to all of the participants. During the workshop, or right afterwards, I jot down a few things about each person I've met so that I can personalize his or her message. Most of the time, I use e-mail, but sometimes I will send notes via regular mail. Just having sent a note is enough to make me stand out from the crowd. Everyone likes to get a note of appreciation.

Being empathetic does not mean changing your personality. Nor does it mean being solicitous or manipulative. It is a positive, sincere, and proactive approach to understanding another's feelings and interests. The dictionary definition of empathy is "the action or understanding, being aware of...the feelings, thoughts, and experience of another...without having the feelings, thoughts, and experience fully communicated in an objective, explicit manner." Therefore, to become empathetic, you need to be aware of communication styles and personality types.

Appreciative

The quality that makes people charismatic networkers is their natural instinct to give sincere appreciation. I believe you can never tell someone thank you too many times when it is done sincerely.

There are many ways to say thank you. There is the handwritten note sent via the US

Postal Service. There is e-mail, which is quick, easy, and immediate. In addition, there is the face-to-face thank you—delivered sincerely with special emphasis on the communication style of the person you are appreciating. You can also show appreciation by sending a gift. I am a big believer in giving gifts and will share some of my techniques and resources when we get to Chapter 7. Saying "thank-you" may seem like simple etiquette, yet it is amazing what it can do for your professional and personal growth as a networker.

A voice mail message I once received confirmed the value of saying thank you. The message was from the CEO of a company for whom I had done some programs. His message was, "I want to thank you and compliment you on the work you've been doing for us. I also would like to share some of the flattering remarks that several of our senior people have for

However, I have found the notes are even more valuable to my networking efforts. I have started to get referrals to other managers in the companies where I do workshops. So I continue the thank-you chain by writing a thank-you to the folks who referred me. Then I got more referrals. I wrote notes to these folks and to the first of those who referred me. And so it goes. I make sure I thank everyone who initially refers me—back to the very first person in the chain.

The thank-you chain is a simple, efficient, and powerful way to show appreciation and to be remembered. I have "thank-you chains" throughout many companies where I work.

you...." While it took the CEO just thirty seconds from his busy day to make this phone call, it had such an impact on me that I kept it on my answering machine for two weeks.

We all strive to be remembered positively by others. Showing sincere appreciation always makes a lasting impression. People want to do business with people they enjoy being with and they will seek them out. In addition, an affirming communication has a way of leading to other opportunities.

Here is how a personal expression of gratitude led to a referral and a new client. After thanking one of my suppliers for helping me meet a near impossible deadline, he said he wanted to do something for me in return. He told me about another client of his who he thought might use my services and he gave me the referral. I followed up and now have a new client. All for a simple thank-you.

Tenacious

At least 20 percent of my business has come from people who turned me down the first time. When I realized this, it was a lesson to me in how being tenacious could pay off for networking and for business.

I remember how one current client was particularly tough to win over. For three years I called this client and got nowhere. Not one call returned. The direct approach clearly was not working, so I decided to network my way to her. What organizations and events, I thought, would she be likely to attend? I belong to several business networking groups I thought might be possible. At least, if the person I was trying to reach might not attend a meeting, perhaps there would be someone from her company who knew her. My break came when I was giving a presentation at a meeting of one of these groups. (More on joining and getting involved in groups in Chapter 6.) After my presentation, a woman from my potential client's company approached and suggested I meet with someone in her company who could use my services. She offered to set up the meeting. Guess who this some-one turned out to be? None other than, Ms. "Never Returns My Calls."

The story does not have a happy ending quite yet. We did meet, and at first, I could tell the woman was doing it out of courtesy for her co-worker and really did not want to meet with me. However, things got better as the meeting progressed, and ultimately went from the twenty minutes she said she had allotted to me to an hour and a half. At the end, she said, "I like your proposal, but frankly, it takes at least five years for outside consul-tants to land a job with our firm. However, you can call me every quarter just to stay in touch." At first I was discouraged, but then I thought, "At least I got in the door!" And now, with five years to go, I'd better hang in there (as my father would say). I sent my thank-you note and a month later when I heard she had been promoted, I sent her a note of congratulations. When the first quarter was up, I called her and left this message, "I know

I still have four and three-quarter years left. I'm just touching base." I continued to keep in touch for another quarter or two, when to my surprise, she called me. She awarded me not one, but two projects with her firm. I have since done over thirty projects with the company. It is one of my largest clients. My tenacity paid off. Rather than getting discouraged about the five-year timetable, I just put on my schedule to call her every quarter and stayed in touch.

There is a fine line between being tenacious and being a pest. Be careful not to cross this line. Much of it has to do with getting permission to keep in touch. In the "five-year case," I knew my initial meeting had gone well and, since she invited me to keep in touch, it was appropriate to follow up with the phone calls and notes. Being tenacious in a positive way means taking advantage of opportunities, as well as looking at the setbacks that come along as opportunities in disguise, and keeping at it.

Enthusiastic and Energetic

Enthusiasm and energy are contagious. When you are enthusiastic, you bring out the enthusiasm in others. If you are full of energy, the energy in the space around you rises. If you do not believe me, watch what happens at a gathering when folks are waiting for a speaker to take the floor. If the speaker arrives with energy, watch how the expressions on the audience's faces change and how the room becomes "charged." Energy and enthusiasm make communication easier. It puts people at ease. It makes people relaxed and receptive to your message.

Realize though that enthusiasm and energy come in many forms. One does not have to be loud and excited to be energetic or enthusiastic. Enthusiasm can be a quiet passion that shines and makes people want to be a part of it.

Caring

I believe when you truly care about others and you don't expect a pay back for your efforts, you will indeed get the ultimate reward. You will make others feel good about themselves and about you.

Often, the act of caring produces unexpected, positive networking results. Recently I received one of those "voice from your past" phone calls. It was from Gloria, who had been

I.A.S.M.

Look at the last four letters in the word enthusIASM—
I Am Sold Myself.

You have to believe in yourself and your ideas first before others will join you.

It's Not about a Quick Hit

You know the pathological networker. This is the individual you see at events passing out his or her cards in a frenzy, obviously there for no other reason than to get a job or make a quick sale. A woman once walked up to me at an event, tapped me on the shoulder, and thrust her card into my hand. "I'm a photographer," she announced, oblivious to the conversation I was having with others. "Call me for work." Needless to say, that brusque introduction did not inspire me to pick up the phone and hire her.

Sadly, her approach is all too common at many functions today.

the receptionist at a company I had called on to sell advertising space years ago. It had been fourteen years since I had last seen her. She was now the vice president of marketing for another company. She had recently read an article of mine and decided to call me about doing a project for her new company. I was quite flattered by her call and her invitation to do a project. When I asked her what made her call me she said, "You always made me feel important whenever you called. Moreover, you even told Jim, our president, that I had a great voice and a smile that truly came across the phone." She was right—I remember when I told him and that was a lifetime ago! She told me how she always remembered my kindness and now she wanted to return the favor. As far as I was concerned, there was no "favor to be returned" for she did have a great voice and I still remember how nice she was to me when I was starting out as a struggling publisher selling ad space. When I complimented her, it was sincere and without a thought of any payback. Yet here it was—fourteen years later!

Effective networkers are always networking not because they "need" to—they network to create lifelong connections with people. They embrace networking as a way of life. They network without the thought of getting an immediate or specific payback. Effective networkers know they are making positive connections in which all parties ultimately benefit. How very different this is from the image many hold of networkers, which is what I call the "pathological networker" who engages in "negative networking." These folks never think of picking up the phone, writing a note, sending an e-mail, or extending a helping hand until they need something. They are not networking.

In Summary

When you have developed and practiced the traits of an effective networker and you suddenly do find yourself out of a job, or need business, you will have no problem contacting people who will be more than glad to lend a helping hand. They will listen, offer sound advice, opportunities, and real referrals. Nonstop networking does work. Make nonstop networking a way of life.

Chapter 5

When Networking Doesn't Come Easy: Networking for Introverts

Nonstop NETWORKING

While having dinner one night with my friends, Karen and John, Karen said to me, "Andrea, you and I are great networkers and John just isn't. We have no problem walking into a room full of perfect strangers, meeting, and having conversations with many folks in the course of an evening. John is content to meet just one or two people and to stay put for the whole evening." As she said this, I looked over at John and saw his face fall. I said, "John is a great networker. He just does it differently than you and I. He has a long list of valuable contacts and he gets many referrals. He helps everyone and they help him. People believe in him and trust him." "You're right," she said. "I just never thought of it that way." She did not realize there are different ways to network. I've seen Karen and John at meetings together. While she "works the room," he is engrossed in conversation with a new contact or a colleague. However, when they walk out of the meeting, they both have contacts, referrals, and leads.

The differences in Karen and John's approaches to networking are a result of their different personality traits. Karen is an extrovert. Extroverts get their energy from being around and interacting with other people. John is an introvert. Introverts gather their energy internally. For example, another friend of mine, Heather, an extrovert, is so wound up and excited after a party or a meeting that her mind races with new ideas and new possibilities that she can't wait to put into action. On the other hand, my friend Suzanne, an introvert, says she is exhausted after such events and longs to refresh and energize herself with a solitary walk on the beach so she can assimilate new ideas.

The Introvert's Networking Advantage

Many introverts, like John, are good networkers. They know how to use their introverted nature to their advantage. For example, John is a good listener; he notices details and remembers important facts. Because he lets others do the talking, they think he is a brilliant conversationalist. He is also a thoughtful person, always the first to give a compliment, to

Characteristics of Introverts and Extroverts

INTROVERTS	EXTROVERTS
Recharged by being alone	Energized by contact with others
Prefers to listen	Talkative
Thoughtful and reflective	Action oriented
Focused	Multitasks
May be mistaken as aloof	Seen as friendly and outgoing
Speaking means is ready to act	Just speaks
Needs time and space for self	Likes to surround self with others
Keeps thoughts to self	Talking is "thinking out loud"
Reacts internally	Reacts externally

remember a special event, and, of course, to say thank-you. A thoughtful person is a remembered person. Because of these positive traits, people trust John and are willing to help him when he needs a favor.

If you are an introvert like John, the first step is to understand your best qualities and learn how to use them to your advantage in networking.

Thoughtful Listener

Listening carefully to others is a skill most extroverts need to work on. It comes easier to introverts who naturally absorb and use what they hear. Introverts generally spend more time listening and less time talking.

One of the best communicators I know is Alice. Every time we meet, she will mention something she remembers about me from a prior conversation. Not long ago, she and I were meeting about a project when she began the conversation with, "How is your sister, Meredith, and her new horse, Noddy?" I was impressed. Not only did she remember my sister's name; but she also remembered she loves her horses!

Alice is one of the best listeners I know; she remembers the details. She puts this skill to work to network effectively. For example, remembering that I mentioned a friend who was looking for a new job, she gave me a contact that she thought might be useful to my friend's job search. Later, when I found out that Alice's company was going through some tough times, I told her about a job opening I thought would be a perfect fit for her skills. I gave her a contact name, she applied for the job, and she is now happily employed. I not only received a lovely thank-you note but also a referral for a speaking engagement with her new company. The referral came with detailed information about the person I was to contact as well as useful information on what materials to send.

Alice is someone who epitomizes what I call a good networker—she listens, she takes in all sorts of information, and when the time is right, she will put different folks and projects together where she thinks there is a good fit. If you asked her, she would tell you she is totally introverted and does not consider herself good at networking. I beg to differ.

Introverts can take advantage of their listening skills to build sound relationships, which is at the heart of being a good networker.

Caring and Helpful

The strengths of the introvert include depth of concentration, comfort with the world of ideas and thoughts, and a caring and helpful attitude towards others. This is a description of my friend, Ken. He is always ready with praise and appreciation for others. When he says something, he has thought carefully before speaking. He is constantly thinking of others. As his wife told me, when they are shopping he is always picking up items that would "be perfect" for others. He not only sends notes of appreciation, but he has a collection of note cards and always picks the one that is "just right" for the occasion and the recipient. He gives freely of his expertise and advice in his profession, and is an active volunteer at his tennis club. He does not consider himself a particularly social person, yet he has many loyal friends who would, and have, helped him out whenever he needed a favor.

I am also reminded of my friend Margie, a small business owner and one of the best networkers I know even though she is a self-proclaimed introvert. Her strength is her helpfulness. One day when I was in need of a certain resource, I called her. Of course, she knew just the right person to call, and within an hour I had what I needed. Because I know and trust her, I'm always quick to refer her and her company and she in turn has referred me and my business—as well as finding me an accountant, a computer consultant, and an insurance carrier!

Introverts network well in situations where they can use their skill to help others.

Passionate

While many introverts don't relish the idea of walking up to a stranger and starting a conversation, when you get them talking on a topic they are passionate about their shyness magically disappears.

When you can focus on an aspect of your business, industry, or a product you are passionate about, you will naturally speak with enthusiasm and conviction. An account executive, Richard, told me he became so nervous before meeting with a prospective client that

Make Networking Work for You and Your Personality

Remind yourself:

- I am prepared and focused
- I am a good listener
- I am passionate about my work
- I am approachable
- I am interested in others and what they have to say
- I am someone whom others trust

he even felt nauseous. Yet as soon as he started speaking about his product, the benefits of which he truly believed, he felt comfortable and at ease.

Introverts need a focus and a genuine reason to make a contact.

Ten Networking Techniques for the Quiet Networker

Under certain circumstances most of us do feel shy, reticent, or introverted, regardless of what label you put on it. Half of us feel shy all the time and others 50 percent of the time. We've all felt stuck in the doorway thinking, "Shall I walk into that crowded room or back to my own hotel room?" Yet we know that the one key component of successful networking is visibility. You can't get that in your hotel room, unless you are networking over the Internet (more on that later).

Networking is about making connections, building relationships, and developing advocates—people who know us and know what we do so that they can become our marketers. Here are ten tips on how to do this even when you are feeling introverted.

1. Have a goal.

Set goals for opportunities you have to expand or to nurture your network.

- ▪ When attending a networking event, set a goal to meet and follow up with at least two people.

- At a company function, set a goal to sit next to someone new. Think of three questions you can ask to learn about what they do, how they got to where they are, and then something personal about them—family, hobby, sports interest.

- Every day, send an e-mail to someone in your Internet address book you have not heard from recently.

- Once a week, go through your contact list and call three people just to say hello.

- Once a month, have lunch with a friend, colleague, or client you have not seen for a while.

2. Take "baby steps."

The concept of networking, or building your network, can be daunting when looked at as a "big picture." However, when you break a project or goal into smaller pieces, you can do it bit by bit. Networking is not a problem for me, but writing a book was! Thinking of the whole project was very scary to me. I had to break it down into baby steps—research, outline, and write one chapter at a time. I set goals and timelines for each part. Were there times when fear overtook me? Sure, and I still moved forward in baby steps. Soon, it was a reality.

Standing in the doorway, a networking event can seem scary. So take it step by step. Start with a hello and a smile. Establish eye contact and

That Reminds Me Of...

Ever wonder how politicians and other celebrities always manage to steer their interviewer back to the topic THEY want to talk about? While it is often the result of some pretty sophisticated and expensive media training, here's a technique you can use at your next networking event to get the same results. The technique is called "bridging." All you have to do is find a word or phrase in the other person's conversation that "reminds you" of what you want to talk about, and bridge back to your topic by saying, "that reminds me of..." Then you will be back on *your* topic.

repeat the name of the person you have just met. Ask an open-ended question, listen to the response, and before you know it you will have made a connection! You can break down the whole concept of building a network using the steps in this book. Just keep taking those baby steps one at a time.

3. Begin with a compliment.

This is a wonderful way to start a conversation. A hairdresser I know who is quiet by nature always finds something complimentary to say about someone to start a conversation. One day he might notice something you are wearing that is particularly flattering, and another day it might be an observation about a lipstick color. Once he commented on my friend's new car as he pulled into the driveway. Starting a dialogue in this way is easy, and everyone likes to get a compliment.

4. Use a script.

If calling to follow up with a new contact makes you a bit nervous, develop a short yet detailed script to use. Write down key points and rehearse it until it comes across naturally. Besides your script, have notes to refer to about the person you are calling. After you do this a few times, it may become second nature to you and you will get by with just your notes. Using a script is a good way to develop confidence.

You can even develop a script for face-to-face meetings at events. Do your homework before the event or meeting and have a list of conversation starters. Then of course you will have your 30-second infomercial polished and rehearsed. Lastly, prepare three "small talk" topics—current events, new movies or books, or industry news.

Most introverted people are well prepared and thorough, so use this characteristic to your advantage in planning for networking encounters.

5. Work on your eye contact.

Recognize the disastrous effect of not making eye contact. Not only does it give the impression you are not listening or paying attention, but the person you are speaking with may consider you rude.

One former client of mine, Ed, is a skilled executive and a thoughtful and caring person. However, his colleagues and employees told me repeatedly they felt that he wasn't listening or giving them his full attention when they spoke. Ed always looked off to the side whenever he was speaking with anyone.

Hallway Schmoozing in Albuquerque

Here's some great advice from Richard Shrout, an indexer by profession, an introvert by nature, and a master networker.

"When you are going to spend your time and money to attend a national or local meeting, take the time beforehand to determine your goals. My own goals for the Albuquerque Conference of the American Society of Indexers, besides learning how to spell "Albuquerque," were the following:

1. Meet in person and spend quality time with an important client's indexing coordinator.
2. Renew friendships with other clients and colleagues.
3. Make some new friends.
4. Muddle through my round-table presentation.
5. Participate in the singing group for the first time.
6. Sell some chapter bumper stickers at random intervals.
7. Help someone just getting started.

Over lunch one day as I was talking and he was looking off to the side, I confronted him. "Ed, I know you're probably not aware of this, yet because you do not look me in the eye when we speak, I feel as though our conversation is not important to you." He protested, saying that our conversation was very important to him. I continued, "Ed, do you realize that most of the time you don't look people in the eye, and in doing this you are communicating exactly the opposite of what you want to communicate, which is that you are listening carefully and respectfully?" He told me he was shy and felt uncomfortable looking people directly in the eye. This feeling is common for shy or introverted people, but the results of not looking someone in the eye are devastating for establishing relationships.

Because eye contact was awkward for Ed, I suggested he try the "third eye approach," which is to look at a spot just above and between someone's eyes. Over time, he became more and more comfortable at looking people right in the eye. The results were amazing. People warmed up to him, his confidence grew, and his network expanded.

6. Attend events with a purpose.

Instead of just going to meetings and events for the general purpose of networking, attend only those events where you have a specific purpose in mind.

A friend of mine told me how he once attended an industry event for the sole purpose of meeting the speaker. The speaker was a prominent leader in his field and my friend was writing a book related to this field and wanted to be able to send it to the speaker for an endorsement when it was finished. Therefore, my friend's goal at this event was to introduce himself to the speaker and establish a reason for a follow-up contact. He didn't care about anything else at this meeting. If he met others in his field, that was a bonus; if the food was good, that was fine

You may have noticed these goals did not include attending classes, round tables, and general presentations. While I did attend most of the conference sessions, my priority was getting to know my colleagues. I call that "schmoozing."

Where does one schmooze? The obvious areas are in the hallways linking the exhibit room and registration area with the presentation rooms, the exhibit room itself, lobby areas, the hotel restaurant, the hospitality suite, and the evening reception. Here are the not so obvious areas—the swimming pool and the workout room, local restaurants and bars, and the back row in general sessions. Areas not conducive to schmoozing include classrooms (with the exception of breaks and total boredom), work sessions, and definitely hotel rooms.

What are the rules of successful schmoozing? The number one rule is very simple: *Be friendly*. In the hallway, make eye contact and talk to those

continued ...

around you. Here is a really big secret. Think of the other person first. Find people who need to meet each other and introduce them. Here's a scary one. Try something new. I tried the singing group in Albuquerque. And I made some great new friends!

Has anyone figured out why my goal number 6—selling bumper stickers—is included? Let me clarify that I hate selling. However, these bumper stickers are funny and sell themselves. But the real secret is the location for selling bumper stickers, which is in the demo/registration area. As a veteran of selling T-shirts at previous conferences, I knew there would be constant opportunities to meet colleagues on friendly, neutral ground.

Here's another important rule of schmoozing; *Be flexible.* Don't let anything else get in the way of your schmoozing goals. For instance, I skipped an entire class on the last day of the conference, but in the process solidified a lifetime friendship with a colleague. What is more important?"

too, but neither interested him. His goal was clear—and he accomplished it.

7. Set up one-on-one meetings.

Next time you go to a networking event, give yourself a goal to connect with just one person and to set up a follow-up, one-on-one meeting. Make this meeting at a comfortable place and time so you can relax and get to know one another. Coffee shops are good venues; no one will rush you and many have comfortable seating arrangements conducive to conversation. It is much easier to get to know someone in this atmosphere than at events and get-togethers.

8. Do your networking at your highest energy level time of day.

Everyone has a time of day when they feel more energized. If possible, set up meetings, make phone calls, and attend events during this high-energy time for you. This may not be possible if you have to attend a meeting in the evening and you are a morning person, but you can still deal with it. Pace yourself during the day (or even take a quick "power nap") to conserve your energy for later when you will need it.

9. Set a time limit.

One "quiet networker" I know gave me this strategy of dealing with networking events. She sets a time limit, saying to herself, "I'll go to the meeting for one hour and then I can go back home and relax." She feels she can successfully gather her energy for an hour, whereas a full evening would be overwhelming. By using this strategy, she gets herself to go to the meetings knowing "it's only for an hour."

Use the same tactic in making calls. Decide how much time you will give to this task and stick to it. Don't be unrealistic, start small—remember to take "baby steps." When you achieve your goal, you'll be energized for the next time.

10. Recharge and reward yourself.

Plan your schedule so that you have time to recharge and reward yourself. Do something

An Introvert's Networking Success Story

E-learning consultant Stu Tanquist shared this story with me:

"Networking did not come naturally to me. Like many introverts, through much of my life I avoided situations involving groups of unfamiliar people. When I started my consulting business, I recognized the importance of networking and knew that I had to change. Most importantly, I needed to get good at initiating conversations with strangers and to feel comfortable mingling in large unfamiliar groups.

I believe that if you want to be good at something, you need to make a study of it. Therefore, I read numerous articles and books and listened to audiotapes on the subject of networking. I took many notes and wore out a few highlighters. I focused primarily on getting past those first few awkward moments and learned the power of asking questions to explore the background, interests, and activities of others.

continued ...

Most importantly, I took action to practice what I had learned and forced myself to attend what I thought would be uncomfortable social situations. I was pleasantly surprised to find that my feelings of discomfort quickly gave way to confidence. I realized that either the people I approached were extroverts who were easy to talk to or they were introverts who were delighted to have someone break the ice and initiate the conversation. Either way, networking became easy. I found myself leaving business meetings completely energized and excited to return.

Today, most people assume that I am an extrovert because they see me actively engaged in social situations, moving from conversation to conversation with comfort. I still consider myself to be an introvert. The difference is that I now actively seek networking opportunities and look forward to attending social functions, even when I know that I won't know a single person."

nice for yourself. Reward yourself for accomplishing each goal you set, and for the completion of each "baby step" along the way. My friend Suzanne—the one who feels drained after networking meetings—treats herself to a long walk, listens to her favorite music, or snuggles in with a good book and a glass of wine. Do whatever works for you, but do something, even if it is just reaching around and giving yourself a well-deserved pat on the back!

Networking on the Internet

Online networking is a new and efficient way to establish relationships with others in your field. Finding and meeting people who can help you with a job search or other networking goal is easy to do with the help of your Internet browser's search engine. You probably already know the important websites in your profession or industry. If you haven't already done so, you can join newsgroups, forums, and other list serves where you can actively exchange ideas and information with others in your field. You can also take classes, workshops, and seminars online. Some industry organizations even have "virtual" events and meetings.

The autonomy of the Internet makes it easier to make new connections. You can "listen" to a discussion group and join in when you feel comfortable. No one will see how nervous you are or notice you standing off in a corner. You can contact almost anyone you want to meet through e-mail. E-mail is easier and faster than playing phone tag, and you do not have to create or practice a script before calling. Just be sure to create an e-mail message that states your purpose clearly and succinctly.

Still another advantage to online networking is the opportunity for you to become a known entity in your own field. No fear of public speaking need deter you in this effort. You can post an article you have written online, you can contribute to a professional website, and you can even create your own website to promote yourself and your business.

It seems that online networking is perfect for introverts and other quiet networkers. There are advantages, for sure, but there are disadvantages as well. Don't kid yourself, online networking can be just as hard as traditional networking. There are rules and conventions for discussion groups and forums. There are technical issues to deal with. These and other issues are beyond the scope of this book. Just realize that online networking it is an option for you to try.

In Summary

When networking doesn't come easily, we may develop negative ideas about what it is and our ability to do it. Networking, as we've said before, is about creating long-lasting relationships that are mutually beneficial. Any and everybody can do it; there is no one "correct way" to network. Introverted or quiet people, when they build upon their strengths, are effective networkers. Develop and follow a process that fits your personality and comfort level and you will be successful.

I like to think of the process as something you can post on your bulletin board or a mirror as a constant reminder.

P–Create a Plan that fits your Personality

O–Do it in an Organized fashion

S–Stick to your own System

T–Remember it takes Time to build relationships

Now you have networking techniques, know the types of people you want in your network, and can develop the characteristics of a good networker. In the next chapter we will look at to how to expand your network.

Chapter 6

How to Expand Your Network

Think of your network as your own ever-evolving "World Wide Web" of contacts and resources you can access for information and links to others. First you have to build your network of "web-sites," and then you have to learn how to get the most out of them. Finally, you need to keep your "web" growing, adding new contacts as some drop away and making sure to nurture all the contacts you worked so hard to make.

In this chapter I'll give you tips on how to expand the network you currently have. It's all about getting the numbers, as you will see. Later we will talk about how to manage and develop the contacts in your network in the most efficient and effective way for you.

To grow your network, you need to take these five action steps:

1. Identify the people who can help you.

Three frogs are sitting on the edge of a pond. One decides to jump in. How many frogs are sitting on the edge?

Did you think, "Two, of course"?

Let me try this again. Three frogs are sitting on the edge of a pond. One decides to jump in. Now how many are sitting on the edge?

The answer is three. One of the frogs decided to jump, but he has not yet jumped. That leaves three frogs still sitting on the edge of the pond.

Don't be left sitting on the edge. Jump into expanding and developing your network.

2. Compare this list to the list you started in Chapter 3, people you know who will take your call.

3. Re-connect with those already in your network, and keep it up as your network grows.

4. Identify the organizations and activities where people you want to know gather.

5. Get involved in these organizations.

Identify the People Who Can Help You

These can be specific individuals or the title of individuals within an organization if you don't know the name of the person who currently holds that position. Aim high. Include high-level executives and celebrities in your field.

Compare This List to the List You Started in Chapter 3

Go back to the list of people already in the network you started in Chapter 3. Remember, these are people who would take your phone call or return it if you called them today. How many of the people you have identified as people who can help you are already in your network? How many may be "six degrees of separation" (or less) away from those who can help you? I'll bet you'll find some people already in your network have good connections. My friend Jeri knows "everyone." She is a board member for a number of organizations, an active member of her church, and a successful professional. She attributes her success to being an active networker herself and to helping others make connections that benefit their careers. She helped me by introducing me to a magazine editor I had identified as someone I wanted to meet. Yes, I could have called directly and might have gotten through over a period of time, but Jeri made it possible faster and with a personal touch. Are there people like Jeri on your list?

Take another look at your bosses and co-workers past and present who are on the list you made in Chapter 3. Have you stayed in touch? Would a note or a call be worthwhile? Are they themselves, or do they know, the people on your list?

What about alumni of your high school or college? I am involved with my college alumni organization and spoke at a recent meeting. The contacts I re-opened there led to opportunities in two new industries for me. Take a closer look at your alumni magazine with an eye toward people who can help you in your profession. My editor's niece, a recent graduate of a leading technical college, launched a successful career as a photographer's stylist in New York City based almost solely on contacts with alumni of her school. She actually knew very few of them prior to coming to the city, but she sought them out and they were willing to help her because they were fellow alumni.

How about neighbors and people who work in your neighborhood? The coffee shop in my neighborhood is a favorite hangout of mine for breakfast with friends, clients, and prospects. I do a lot of networking there. The manager, Jose, always asks me how I'm doing, and over the years we've gotten to know each other. Recently he proudly showed me a magazine with an article of mine. He has introduced me to several people who he thought I should know. He was right! I've met some great new business contacts through him and I tell everyone I meet about the best coffee shop in New York—The Madison Restaurant at 53rd and First Avenue.

Did you list any competitors? A decorator friend of mine tells me the story of how losing the bid for a project turned into a networking opportunity with her competition. Although she had lost the bid for the design, she did win the contract to write the project and ended up working closely with the winning decorator. They worked so well together that they decided to team up for future projects. Five years later they have contracts and large national accounts together that might not have happened if they had worked independently.

Re-connect with Those Already in Your Network

Make a game plan for re-connecting with those already in your network who can help you. The people on the list you made in Chapter 3 will take your phone call. Here's the opportunity to give them a call. "For what reason?" you ask. No reason, just to touch base. To say hello. To catch up on what has been happening in your lives.

Don't be shy, people love to get these calls. They may have been thinking of and meaning to call you. These calls are especially easy to make because you are not going to be asking for anything. Although if you have not been in touch for a while you might expect a reaction like, "What do you want?" Imagine their surprise and pleasure when they realize it is just a friendly call.

Here's a game plan you can try. I call it my **FOUR**-mula for Success. Call four people per week from your list.

1. A client or prospect you have not been in touch with for a while

2. A former business colleague

3. A former friend

4. A current friend

The last call, to a current friend, will be the easiest, most fun, and a reward for making the other three. As you work through your list, over time you will find that all four calls have become "current." Then, you just keep it going. It is easy to fit four calls a week into your busy schedule. It breaks down the formidable task of re-connecting with your list into manageable, bite-sized tasks—baby steps. And it will become a practice you continue to use as your network grows. Most important will be the results. Imagine how easy it will be to ask for a favor now that you have solidified your relationship.

Identify the Organizations Where People You Want to Know Gather

Think of the places, events, associations, trade organizations, and conferences where people in your profession, or one that you are interested in, get together to exchange information, contacts, knowledge, or just to enjoy each other's company. Make a list. What do you already know about these organizations? Do you belong and attend meetings? Would you like to know more about these and find others that will help you build your network?

Chances are you know the best organizations for your own profession. But if you are just starting out, changing careers, or want to find more resources, the following is a short course in how to identify and locate groups and formats that offer networking opportunities.

Types of Networking Groups

Basically, there are four types of networking groups categorized by purpose: general networking, industry specific, service, and special interest.

- **General Networking** groups are groups where the primary, stated purpose is to network and to exchange leads, contacts, and tips. Most are not industry specific. Some better known ones arc:

    Business Network International (BNI) www.bni.com

    Leads Club www.leadsclub.com

    Le Tip International, Inc. www.letip.com

    National Association of Female Executives (NAFE) www.nafe.com

Here is an example of how one of these groups works. Business Network International is a national organization with chapters in most cities. Each chapter has from ten to thirty members, each from a different profession or industry. In fact, there can only be one member in a given

Networking Down Under

This from a colleague, Julie, in Australia:

"Here in Newcastle, New South Wales, Australia, we have what we call a 'Tag Team.' When women, working for ourselves, come across an opportunity, they will make a referral to another woman in the group. We have started a group for this activity called Fishnets—fishing for business via networking. No, we don't wear fishnet stockings!

The tag team concept works very well and helps us make strategic alliances outside the group. It works well because of the following reasons:

■ A referral comes pre-endorsed to the customer.

profession or industry in a chapter; for example, one accountant, one real estate agent, one decorator, one stock broker, and so on.

Meetings are typically held early in the morning before business hours and last about an hour. Members give a 30-second talk about their business and the type of clients they hope to find. (Here's where you can use your 30-second infomercial.) The idea is that others in the group become familiar enough with each other's business that they will refer clients. For example, you attend a BNI meeting, give your presentation, and hear others. Later, at a neighborhood get-together, your neighbor mentions he wants to re-finance his home mortgage but has lots of questions about how to go about it. A member of your BNI group is a mortgage banker. You mention him to your neighbor and ask if it would be okay if he gave your neighbor a call. Perhaps he could answer his questions. You have made a referral.

At each meeting, you report the referrals you have made for your colleagues. The purpose of this organization is to help each other. If a member is only getting referrals and not giving them, his efforts are questioned and he may be asked to resign from the group. Members are encouraged to get to know one another, to meet, and to network outside the meetings as well. Also, at each meeting one member has the opportunity to make a longer (about fifteen minutes) presentation about his business. In addition, the coordinator of the group will offer networking tips.

Reported results are mixed. People who belong to these groups and work hard at helping each other get lots of referrals and make lots of beneficial contacts. It is like anything else in networking: you get what you give.

People who belong to these groups are there to network. Therefore, starting a conversation and delivering your 30-second infomercial

■ You work doubly hard to look after the customer you have been referred to because you do not want to disappoint the person who referred you or the team.

Newcastle is like a big county (it is the fifth largest city in Australia) and nearly all business is word of mouth.

Incidentally, all but the original two of us (long-term friends both from Sydney) met at networking meetings. Our group never set out to be exclusively for women, but so far we haven't needed to call on any 'blokes.' (Some of us, including myself, however, sub-contract to some.)"

should be easy for you in these meetings. To find out more information and for local chapter information, go to the websites mentioned. To find more groups like these check your local Yellow Pages under Business and Trade Associations. You will have to ask questions to determine the specific purpose of organizations under this listing.

■ **Industry Specific** organizations are groups organized around a specific industry or profession. Although a lot of networking goes on, networking is not the major purpose. It may be educational, informational, or, as in the case of some trade associations, regulatory. Most are open to those who work in, or who aspire to work in, the industry or profession they represent. Others are private and exclusive, requiring specific qualifications and recommendations from current members. All provide a wide variety of services to members, not the least of which is the opportunity to meet and greet like-minded people.

I have long been an active member of the Direct Marketing Association, the premier association of the industry where I built my career. Through the years, I have found clients, suppliers, friends, mentors, and even my "significant other." (Talk about like-minded people!) Early in my career, I identified an individual I wanted to know, Lee Epstein, known as the "godfather of direct marketing." Because I was active in this organization, I came to meet him. We became friends, and he and his wife, Rose, have also been wonderful mentors to me in this business. Working together with him and others in this organization has opened many doors for me through the years.

You can find these groups and trade associations easily by asking others in your business or profession or by reading trade magazines. Many have local chapters, which you will find in your Yellow Pages. Or, you can look in the *American Society of Association Executives Directory*. This directory lists well over 20,000 such organizations with contact information, including websites. You can find this reference book at your local public library.

Joining and becoming active in one or several of these groups will provide you with many profitable networking opportunities and will be a boost to your career.

Finding T

Associa

Here is a way to find trade associations for your industry using Google, a popular and effective Internet search engine. First, to access Google, go to www.google.com. Then, in the tool bar above Google search, click on directory. On the page that comes up, click on the "business" category. Then you will see a lot of categories. Find and click on "associations." Then click on "trade associations." You will see more categories. Click on a category that best describes your industry or profession. For example, clicking on "marketing" will give you a list of marketing associations including the Direct Marketing Association, mentioned in this chapter

■ **Service Groups.** There are many public, private, and charitable organizations with members from various walks of life that exist for the purpose of providing service to others. Some of these include:

Rotary Clubs

Lions

Kiwanis

Chambers of Commerce

Political clubs such as Democratic or Republican Clubs

The League of Women Voters

Charitable or fund raising groups

Church groups

PTAs

Plus various other civic and community groups, including your neighborhood homeowners association.

Whether you belong to any of these and use them as a networking resource is dependent upon your interest and inclination to volunteer your time and expertise to your community. These groups exist to serve the community, not for networking. However, as I have said, like-minded people are people you want in your network. And you will find these people here. You will also find caring people, often one and the same as effective networkers, as we mentioned in Chapter 4. In addition, at many charitable and fund raising events you will find executives and other business leaders who volunteer their time and name to these events. What better way to get to know them and for them to get to know your abilities, than to work on such an event. So by all means join, volunteer, and profit from these organizations.

Amy owns a small public relations company and is also an art enthusiast. She is on the board of a local museum and recently volunteered to chair a major fund raising event for the museum. She was in contact with many business executives and leaders to solicit donations for the event and to sell tickets. She had a very high profile job as chairperson of the event, and she met many influential people. They got a first-hand look at her abilities as a public relations professional. The event was an enormous success and there is no doubt the contacts Amy made will serve her well in her business.

■ **Special Interest** groups are the most overlooked in terms of networking opportunities, yet can be the most profitable it you keep your eyes and ears open. These are the fun groups and events. Your health club, book club, bridge club, gourmet-cooking class, pick-up basketball game, Friday evening tennis mixer, even your Alaskan cruise.

All are fun things, but how do they help you make connections? I recall a friend expressing concern about an organized tour of Europe she was about to embark on. "What if I don't like the people? I'm stuck!" " Of course you will like them," I replied. "They enjoy the same things you do or they would not have signed up for this particular tour." I was right. She had a great time and came back with several new friends and professional contacts.

You're never too busy to join these groups and enjoy these events. Keep yourself open to meet new and interesting people. Use the networking techniques from Chapter 2 to make connections and build relationships from these opportunities.

Get Involved

Here is a three-step process to grow your network through involvement with organizations where people you want to know gather.

1. Go to meetings, meet people, and then join the organization(s) best for you.

2. Volunteer, join a committee, become active.

3. Write an article, give a speech, become known.

Go to Meetings, Meet People, and Join the Organization(s) Best For You

As you will discover when researching the groups above, there are a lot of organizations and activities for profitable networking. The trick is to find the ones best for you. Most organizations will encourage a prospective member to attend a couple of meetings before joining. I highly recommend this, no matter what you think you may already know about the organization. Use your networking techniques and set a goal to meet at least two new people at each meeting you attend. Then set a follow-up meeting with each of the people you met to get to know them and to find out more about the organization.

Be sure to ask if the meetings you attended are typical of most meetings. Find out who generally attends meetings. Sometimes, the roster of an organization will include some of the people you want to meet but they may never attend a meeting. Sometimes, the meetings are the wrong environment for you to achieve your goals in your limited time. Yes, it is true you should always be open to connecting with people; however, you also have to make the most of your resources—your time and money. It is important to pick the organizations that work best for you.

My 2-2-2 Strategy

Before you decide to join a group:

Attend two meetings

Meet two people and exchange business cards

Arrange two follow-up meetings for breakfast, lunch, or coffee.

This does two things:

You will find out if you want to join the organization, and

You will expand your network by two.

Ask to see a list of past and future programs. Are these of interest and benefit to you? Are the speakers people you want to hear and meet? Are there other programs and workshops offered that would be of interest and that would help you in your profession? Is there a newsletter? A website? Is it useful and informative? Would you have something to contribute to a newsletter or a program?

For each group or activity you consider, ask yourself:

■ Who attends meetings and actively participates? Are these the people I want to meet?

■ Is the group "network friendly," willing to give and share information with others?

■ Are the meetings, speakers, and activities of interest and benefit to me?

Once you are satisfied with the answers to these questions, then sign up! Join and become an active member.

Volunteer, Join a Committee, Become Active

When you are involved, you will meet more people, make more contacts, get to know the organization better, and your network will expand faster.

Volunteer to be the "greeter" when people are registering for a meeting. This is a great way to meet people. The greeter meets everyone who attends the meeting, so you will be sure to have introduced yourself to those you want to meet. Then you will have an "opening line" to connect with them again later in the meeting.

Join a committee. If you just attend meetings, you will limit your ability to meet and get to know members of the organization. After all, the majority of the time spent at a meeting is devoted to the program. What you want to do is expand your network, not just listen to a speaker, even a good speaker. So, volunteer for a committee or a project that interests you. You will meet and get to know more people faster.

One of the most interesting committees and profitable committees for which to volunteer in an organization is the program committee. As an active member of this committee, you get to meet and interact with all the speakers and presenters—the experts in your field. Is there an important person in your industry you would like to meet but have no logical way to do so? Invite him or her to do a program for your organization. You are now on this person's radar screen (if not in his or her Rolodex).

Become active in the organizations you join. It will expand your network quickly and efficiently.

Write an Article, Give a Speech, Become Known

Remember, before you joined you checked out the organization's newsletter

The World's Shortest and Most Effective Networking Strategy

Answer the following questions:

- Who are the people I'd most like to meet?

- Who knows the most about my industry?

- How can I get in touch with these people?

Through people I know?

Through organizations I belong to?

Who are the four people I'm calling this week? (**FOUR**-mula for Success)

1.

2.

3.

4.

and website with the thought of whether you could make a contribution. Now you have had the chance to learn about the type of articles that are published in the newsletter or on the website and it is time to make that contribution. So, write an article and submit it to the editor or webmaster. Even if you just volunteer to write the recap of the last meeting, write it, get a byline, and get it published. You will become known. It will be easier to meet people when they remember your article. In addition, you will be making a valued contribution to the organization and its members.

Another way to become known and therefore meet more people is to give a speech or presentation for your organization. Organizations are always looking for programs or breakout sessions for larger meetings or conventions. Seize the opportunity to become a presenter. If you are fearful of public speaking, take a course in presentation skills and practice

Summary

What we have seen in this chapter is that in order to expand your network you have to create the opportunities to keep it growing. Identify the people you want to meet and to know. Examine your existing network and re-connect with those with whom you have been out of touch. Then keep it up. It is as simple as four phone calls a week.

Look for the places you are likely to find the people you want to meet. Research and join organizations where they might gather. Don't limit yourself just to networking groups and industry organizations. Think about community service and special interest groups as well. Become active in these organizations, and become known. The more people who know who you are, the more people you have the opportunity to meet. Soon, you will have a large list of contacts who will not only take your phone call, but will be glad to hear from you and glad to help you.

To keep these contacts requires time, attention, and follow-up. In the next chapter, you will learn how to nurture these contacts, creating connections that last a lifetime.

what you've learned whenever you have an opportunity. T[...]
in front of a group, as scary as it is to some of us, is in[...]
skill in today's business world. I have been teaching pres[...]
over fifteen years to hundreds of clients and thousands of[...]
and I can honestly say that learning and practicing these[...]
most of any skill I know of to boost confidence and ensur[...]

A speech or presentation can be as simple as teach[...]
topic you know a lot about. A photographer friend of mine [...]
raphy classes at a local community center and as a result[...]
and referrals for his portrait studio. I teach a class through[...]
education department at New York University called "*Self M[...]
to Z." My class members come from many different professi[...]
tries. For example, last semester my class included a tax[...]
major consulting firm, the owner of a mid-sized advertis[...]
woman who had worked in the film industry, two people fro[...]
tions firms, two from a large cosmetic company, an interna[...]
and an editor of a lifestyle magazine. It was wonderful to se[...]
making connections among themselves. It was truly like-minde[...]
ting together. However, I felt like I was the real winner in all o[...]
class, like so many others I've taught, I made friends a[...]
connections. My network expanded.

Chapter 7

Keeping Your Network Alive and Growing

Now you have been at this for a while. You have conquered your fears, you have confidence, you walk into networking meetings with a goal of meeting and following up with at least two new people, and it is working. Good for you! You have collected a stack of business cards and are now the proud owner of a loaded Rolodex. Now you have to figure out how to keep it all going. "How," you wonder, "do I keep in touch with these folks and nurture the relationships I have started?"

In this chapter, I will show you how to keep in touch with those in your network and build long-lasting mutually beneficial relationships.

As in any relationship, the first thing you will want to do is to get to know the other person's interests, family, and important events. Then, you will want to find ways to keep in touch. This includes the important and

A tip to avoid endless telephone tag is to set up a telephone appointment. Then be sure to be at your phone when you say you will be available.

effective thank-you note. One of the most profitable ways to keep in touch is to become a resource for others. Finally, there is the issue of how to make sure you touch base with everyone on your list on a regular basis.

Getting To Know You

All relationships begin with a "getting to know you" phase. Moreover, most relationships endure because we continue to stay in touch. Remember the list of contacts you made in Chapter 3, those people who would take your phone call? Getting to know a contact gives you information you can use to stay in touch, so that everyone in your network will become a contact for life.

Find Out the Best Way to Stay in Touch

When you meet someone you want to stay in contact with, one of the first things you will want to ask is, "What is the best way for us to keep in touch?" Everyone has a preferred method of correspondence. Some people like the telephone. Even if they cannot take a call, voice mail works for them. I have carried on full conversations with people by exchanging voice mail messages.

Other folks like e-mail and are very good at responding quickly, as you should be also. I know one person who rarely returns phone calls. She knows she should, yet for some reason she rarely does. However, as soon as she receives an e-mail, she responds immediately. Therefore, I know exactly how to communicate with her. In my database I have an "e" for e-mail next to her name. On the other hand, another man I know will never use e-mail. He even told me, "I don't 'do' e-mail." While I cannot understand this attitude in today's world, I clearly know how to communicate with him. He returns every call he gets. I put a "v" for voice next to his name.

The important thing is to ask your contact their preference and then use it when corresponding with them.

Note Important Dates and Anniversaries

Find out important dates and events, birthdays, anniversaries, and other important occasions. Knowing these provides an opportunity to get in touch with a card, e-mail, or phone call. I always ask about birthdays, not necessarily the specific date, but the month. I will ask a contact, "What month where you born in?" or even, "What is your astrological sign?" (Yes, a little corny, but it works.) Then I record this month in my database. I have a list of birthdays for each month and can send out cards for that month all on one date. It does not matter if I miss the exact date; remembering is the important thing.

Anniversaries and important events are also opportunities to keep in touch. Be alert to what people mention about these dates. Some people are proud of work anniversaries: one, five, ten, or more years at their company. Send a note of congratulations on these occasions. Others will mention an upcoming award, honor, or promotion. Or, you may find out about this from co-workers or from an article in a trade publication. Be sure to send a note or even a small gift (more on gifts later).

Family, Interests, and Hobbies

Ask your contacts about their family, interests, and hobbies. One young man I have worked with really goes out of his way to learn about people and their interests. When Pete takes a new job, one of the first things he does is draw a map of his new office area with each cubicle and office. As he meets people, he writes their name on the corresponding space on his map, along with interesting things he learns about them in conversation: names of kids, favorite vacation spots, sports and other interests, favorite restaurants, as well as work information. Pete is creating the foundation for strong business relationships with these people as he starts out in his new job. Finding out the interests of people in your network does several things to build the relationship:

1. **Provides conversation starters.** Everybody likes to talk about himself or herself.

2. **Provides information.** Information you can use to keep in touch.

3. **Provides ideas.** Ideas you can use to become a resource.

Ways To Keep in Touch and Show Appreciation

Now that you are armed with information, here are some ways to use it to keep in touch and build your relationships.

Send a Handwritten Note

The art of writing notes is sadly disappearing. The post office reports that only four percent of mail is personal correspondence. When you open your mailbox a handwritten envelope stands out among the bills and advertise-

Many successful people have employed the personal note as a means of staying in touch and showing appreciation— President George Bush, the Pope, Jack Welch, and Leonard Lauder, to name a few. (They are all great networkers too!)

Thank You for Your Thank-You Note

Here's how a thank-you note paid off. Keith is taking a class in an industry he hopes to break into as a freelancer. Not only is he working hard at improving his skills so he can go out on his own, he is at the same time building a network in his new industry. He sent a hand-written thank-you note to the instructor of the class he recently took. Several days later, he received an e-mail from her, thanking him for his thank-you note! That is not all. She invited him to an upcoming meeting that some important folks in his new industry would be attending. This provided Keith a great opportunity to expand his network. All for a simple thank-you.

ments. "Wow! A real letter—someone is thinking of me." A personal note is the nicest way to connect and re-connect with others and make them feel good.

Thank-You Notes

One of the best and least expensive public relations tools you can use is a simple thank-you note. As discussed in Chapter 4, you can never say, "Thank you" too many times as long as it is sincere.

Here are seven reasons to send a thank-you note:

1. For time and consideration

2. For a compliment you received

3. For a piece of advice given

4. For business

5. For a referral

6. For a gift

7. For help on a project

Always carry notes and stamps with you. Then whenever you have some "found time" in an airport, on a train, waiting at a doctor's office, or watching TV, you can dash off a note, address it, and pop it in the mail.

Don't know what to say? Look in Appendix 2 of this book for some sample notes you can use or that may generate some ideas for you.

Other Notes

Besides the thank-you note, here are several other types of notes you can send at any time to stay in touch and be helpful.

- **"FYI" (For your information).** Send articles or clippings that may be of interest to people in your network. These can be related to their business or personal interests. Include a brief, "I thought of you when I saw this and thought you would enjoy (find it useful, be interested In, or want to havc this for your files)" note. Consider including your business card if the contact is new. It reinforces who you are.

- **"Congratulations!"** For a new job, a promotion, an award or honor, or an anniversary. This is a perfect opportunity to keep in touch.

- **"Nice talking to (or, meeting) you."** I send these notes after a phone conversation (especially a phone appointment or conference call), a meeting, a chance encounter and conversation, and always after meeting someone new at an event or meeting.

■ **"Thinking of you."** I send this for no particular reason other than to stay in touch. It is an easy one, as you can buy a card with this sentiment and just add a brief note. (The card store people love me—I'm always buying cards, see below also.) Sometimes I send this card to people in my network that I have not been in touch with for a while. Often, it reopens the relationship. Whomever you send this to will appreciate it.

Holidays

I send Christmas or Seasons Greetings cards to everyone in my network. I use other occasions to remember and stay in touch as well. I will think about the profile and interests of my contact when sending these. Think about your contacts. Could you send Thanksgiving, Easter, St. Patrick's Day, even Halloween greetings? How about Mother's Day or Father's Day? And the card industry has plenty of others: Friendship Week, Administrator's Week, Grandparents' Week—all opportunities to stay in touch.

"The Power Of Three" Personal Note Plan

You may be thinking, "This is a lot of notes and cards! Who has time?" Let me share with you a technique I adopted and have used successfully for years. It is easy, and does not take much time from your busy day. Moreover, I can assure you from experience that it will pay off in building solid relationships.

Everyday, send three hand-written notes. Make them short notes to express any of the messages above.

Some folks you can send these notes to include:

■ Co-worker

■ Prospect

■ Client

■ Friend

■ Service provider

■ Family member

If you write and send just three notes a day by the end of the workweek you will have connected with 15 people and by the end of the year, 750 (assuming you take a two-week vacation). Try to make these handwritten personal notes in addition to the thank-you and follow-up notes you would normally send.

Writing these notes should take no more than ten minutes a day. You can write them either first thing in the morning before your workday begins or after your workday ends. Writing notes is easy once you get in the habit. Your note does not have to be perfectly crafted; it is the thought that counts. Look in appendix 2 for some sample notes to use.

Once you get the hang of this technique, add a multiplier. Send a total of:

■ Three extra notes,

■ Three extra e-mails, and

■ Three extra phone calls per week.

That is 2,250 connections in a year! I do this and find it to be a great system to continually stay in touch with my contacts.

The goal of making these additional contacts is to build and strengthen your networking "World Wide Web."

Take Full Advantage of E-mail

The hand-written note is a special touch. However, in today's world we are fortunate to have a way to be in instant contact with so many people—all around the world, too. In fact, there is very little excuse for not showing appreciation or following up in a timely fashion with e-mail. It is perfectly appropriate to send a thank-you note for any of the seven reasons mentioned earlier via e-mail. It is also fine to send an article of interest as an e-mail attachment. Just be careful and do not bombard your contacts with articles, notices, or (shudder!) chain letters that are making the rounds on the Internet. Remember, you are extending a professional courtesy and the message should be tailored to the recipient, not be a mass mailing. Make sure you have a valid reason to send the information and always include a personal note. We will talk about networking etiquette in the next chapter, but for now remember to follow one fast rule about e-mail correspondence. Always reply to e-mails within 48 hours of receipt. Not responding quickly makes you appear uninterested and even rude.

Send Gifts To Show Your Appreciation

Sometimes it is appropriate to show appreciation with a gift. Sending a gift sets you apart. When is it appropriate to send a gift? I often send gifts after a project is completed, when someone is promoted, for a birthday or holiday, or when someone has done me a special favor. In a business situation, you need to be careful about the nature of the gift. Keep in mind this is a gesture of appreciation and you do not want to place the recipient in the awkward position of having to turn down your gift due to company policy. In general, food is best in this situation. Most companies that do not allow gifts to employees will allow a gift of food that can be shared with all. Some good choices include a fruit basket, a popcorn tin, or a box of candy or other goodies.

Make your gift stand out. Take the time to develop relationships with special vendors who provide unique products and good service.

Send Out Your Own Articles or Even Create a Newsletter

Besides clipping and sending articles of interest to folks in your network, you can send out your own articles. Perhaps you have published an article in a trade publication or even in a newsletter (a tip from Chapter 5). Copy and send these out with a note.

If you have not published any articles, publish one yourself. Pick out some nice paper at Kinko's, write an article of interest, print it out, and send it off to your network. Or send it electronically.

My quarterly newsletter started this way. After I wrote several articles, I compiled them into a newsletter with tips and techniques on networking, presentation skills, sales, and customer service. It is a short, easy-to-read newsletter that I hope is helpful to all who receive it. I send it to everyone in my network with a brief personal note. It is a great way to keep in touch.

Using Premiums

If you own a business and are networking to expand your client list, invest in premiums with your company's name. I always keep a host of premiums with me to give to folks I meet or who attend my seminars. Each premium has my name, company, and contact information, including my website. Most importantly, all my premiums are useful. The mirror I mentioned in an earlier chapter is my "signature piece." I also have a pen to write notes, candy in a refillable container, magnets for notes on the fridge (or filing cabinet), a pewter paperweight in the shape of a map of the US, and my latest addition, a light bulb filled with mints that says "a bright idea" and my company's name. Think of items that will not only make you memorable, but will stay in front of people as they go about their normal working day. One of my favorites is a small measuring tape that I use often. I see the name of the company who sent it every time I use it.

Whenever I do a project for a company, I call up my friends in the popcorn business and they send out a huge tin of delicious popcorn with a personal note from me. People love it, and when the popcorn is gone, they fight over who gets to keep the tin.

Another one of my favorite vendors is a fruit and pastry company that sends out the most wonderful goodie baskets. I met them over the Internet when they e-mailed me to ask permission to use one of my articles in their newsletter. I was happy to do so and was in the market for a gift basket so I tried them. (Pretty clever networking on their part!)

Another one of my food gifts is candy. I use several places from all over the country that provide mouth-watering candies from caramels to chocolates. Be creative with your food gifts. I have sent everything from chocolate telephones to fruit-flavored flowers.

Of course, when your food gift is shared

with others in the company, your name gets in front of others—an added bonus.

If you can send a more personal gift, then consider the interests of the person you are sending it to just as you would with a gift to a friend or relative.

One friend told me that every time a client visited his office, she always read one particular magazine he had on the coffee table. As a holiday gift, he gave her a subscription to it. On another occasion, after one of his clients referred a piece of business to him, he picked out a special bottle of wine the client had spoken about (both had a strong interest in wines). Gifts are even more special when you take the time to make them personal according to the person's interests. It says you put extra effort into your expression of appreciation.

Note: You will find names and contact information for a few of my favorite gift and premium vendors in Appendix 3.

How To Make Your Name "Stick"

Here's a new and useful calling card that will have folks looking at your name and business every time they open their refrigerator door. Magna Cards are business-card-sized magnets that you can affix your card to and hand out to your contacts. You will find them in office supply stores like Office Depot or Staples. They are a low cost and effective way to make your name "stick."

Follow-up: The Key to Keeping Your Network Alive and Growing

You can be the master of working a room and leave each networking event with a pocket full of business cards, but if you do not follow up with these people and others already in your network, you will never be successful at networking. Follow-up is the key.

When should you follow up?

There are four absolute must-follow-up situations. When you follow up in these situations and in the prescribed time suggested, you will be successful at creating and maintaining an active list of contacts who trust and respect you and who will gladly help you out when you find the need to ask. Here are the situations and how to follow up:

1. Within twenty-four hours after a meeting, send a note, e-mail, or phone to say any of the following, depending upon the circumstances of your meeting:

■ How nice it was to meet.

■ Thank you for your time and consideration.

■ Suggest meeting again.

■ Thank you for the useful information.

This is not only a courtesy, but it will also differentiate you from the myriad of others your contact may have met.

2. If you have promised to send materials, phone to set up a meeting, or pass on a referral, keep your word and do it within the time promised or sooner. It is easy to make these promises at a meeting or event, but it is the person who follows up in a timely manner who is remembered and trusted.

3. Call within two weeks after having made a suggestion to get together, whether over a meal or at a more formal meeting. Just saying, "Let's do lunch" is not an effective networking technique. Don't suggest it unless you mean it, then follow up to set a specific date and place. Twenty-four hours before your get together, call again to confirm. When you follow up in this manner, you will be perceived as being both sincere and professional.

4. If a contact gives you a referral, or offers to pass on your resume or other materials in order to help you out, be sure to thank your contact and let them know the results. You should also do this for any tangible advice given to you from a contact. People who offer help to you in whatever form deserve to know the results of their advice. More importantly, they absolutely deserve a thank-you.

Recently, a friend of mine told me how she not only offered to send a resume of a contact to the company she worked for, but she also spent some time with her contact crafting her resume to what she knew the position required. Not only did she not receive a thank-you, but also she never heard the results. She was disappointed. When the contact called her again to ask if there were any other places she could recommend sending her resume, my friend was not as forthcoming as she might have been.

Following up not only shows good communications skills, but also builds solid relationships for the future and shows respect for others. It helps people remember you and makes them willing to help you.

Become a Resource for Others

Share your skills and experience happy in the knowledge that you are helping friends and colleagues. Others appreciate and seek out knowledgeable people who give generously of their expertise. And when you have been a resource to others, people are more than willing to help you when you ask.

My client Joan is a good example of this. Joan is a resource for everything from a good printer to a good hairdresser. She always goes out of her way to help others, and when someone needs something they call Joan. It was no surprise that when she lost her job due to a downsizing a few years ago, she only had to make two calls to some pals and she was back at work in no time—with a better and more prestigious position. It was easy for her to ask for a favor since she is consistently helpful to others.

Face Time

When you can spend time with someone in person, it is always more powerful and memorable then carrying on a correspondence by phone or e-mail. In today's busy world, it is increasingly difficult to find the time to plan and do this. Distance is also a factor. I have found that if I plan to spend time with certain people in my network, I will manage to do it. There are people in my network who I plan face-to-face meetings with at least once a quarter; others, I plan to see only twice a year, mostly because of distance. Other closer friends and associates I see more frequently.

I have found that you have to be both persistent and creative to make sure you get this face time. Besides the traditional meetings at breakfast, lunch, and dinner, suggest meeting for coffee. Coffee shops seem to be the net-

Make F.A.C.E. Time Work for You

F–Make it Fun. Find unique things to do and places to meet.

A–Adapt to each other's timetable and surroundings.

C–Connect and find common interests.

E–Know when to Exit—be respectful of each other's time.

working place of choice these days. Or try the following: play a game of tennis or golf, go for a walk, meet at a museum, attend an industry event, or get tickets to a play, concert, or sporting event. Even try sharing a cab to a meeting, or meet at the sky club at the airport when you are between flights in your colleague's city. Be creative. Everybody is busy and appreciates new and unique suggestions. Be persistent. A face-to-face meeting is invaluable in building solid relationships.

A Plan to Keep in Touch with Everyone in Your Growing Network

As your network continues to grow, you will want to have a system to stay in touch with each of your contacts. I am frequently asked how I keep in touch with each of the 2,500 people that are on my networking list. Here is how I do it:

I divide my list into three categories: A, B, and C, and I have a contact plan for each category.

The "C" list consists of my "touch-base" people. These are casual acquaintances, interesting people with whom I would like to stay in touch, yet am not immediately involved with on a business or personal level. They may also be former clients or part of a "thank-you" chain. I send each of them my quarterly newsletter (with a short personal note) and once or twice a year, I send a card or note. I also send them a holiday card in December.

My "B" list are "associates." These are people with whom I am actively involved, either professionally or personally. I find a way to meet each of these folks in person, for a meal, tea, or coffee at least two times a year. In addition, I will send them at least six personal notes in a year. If they are out of town and seeing them in person is problematic, I call them every other month to say hello. These people also get my holiday and premium gifts. I also send them my newsletter and a holiday card.

My "A" list are "close friends and associates." I make a point to see each of them at least four times a year for a meal or a longer get together if possible. I send them special gifts and frequent personal notes. In addition, I will actively look for and send articles of interest to them. I also send them my newsletters, holiday cards, and premiums. Also, I look for opportunities to send flowers, theater tickets, or dinner certificates. I constantly think of ways to stay in touch with these people.

These categories are not static by any means. First, the total number of people in my network grows every day of my life. I add these to the appropriate category. Then, I move people from C to B to A and sometimes vice versa depending on what is going on in my life and what my goals are at the time. Sometimes there is a D list, which includes people no longer in my life. These may disappear entirely from my network for a period of time or forever. My goals and life have changed and so have theirs. It is nothing personal. It is similar to cleaning out your closet. Clothes you may have worn and enjoyed in previous years no longer fit your lifestyle (or, no longer fit, period!) To keep your life in focus, you periodically need to eliminate some things from it.

In Summary

In this chapter, I've talked about how to keep a network alive and growing. You have to nurture and tend to your network much the way a gardener tends to his garden. First you plant seeds, then water and feed the growing plants, and then hopefully, they will blossom. For your network, first you make the contact, then you follow up, become a resource, stay in touch, and hopefully, you create relationships that grow and are mutually beneficial. Your network, just like a garden, will only grow and prosper if you take the time to tend to it carefully.

As in any social or business discourse, there are rules of etiquette and conventional behavior that should be observed. Sadly, in today's results driven world, many of these rules and conventions are ignored. I call this phenomenon "Negative Networking." Not only is it rude, it just doesn't work. The next chapter is a review of these rules of etiquette and some examples of how to avoid negative networking.

Chapter 8

Networking Etiquette

While attending a wedding reception last year I thought it was strange when the guest seated across from me at the dinner began distributing his business cards. At first, I just thought he was being friendly and outgoing. However, I was shocked when this fellow, a stockbroker, began asking everyone at the table questions about their investments, making notes, and even bragging that he could get us better returns. Then he called me the next day asking for a meeting and for referrals. I later found out he made the same call to almost everyone who had been at our table.

This was truly poor networking etiquette—negative networking, as I call it. Networking is all about establishing relationships and building trust. This man started working on us before we even got to the soup! Not only did he not bother to get to know us, but he also

Q At a business meal, when can I start the business discussion?

A Business may be discussed after the entrée plates have been removed. Use the time before that to get to know others through conversation starters and open-ended questions.

Q After an interview, is it appropriate to e-mail a thank-you note?

A It is better to send a hand-written note. E-mail is immediate, yet a hand-written note shows you care and makes you stand out.

Q I'm expecting an important call. Do I leave my cell phone on during a networking meeting?

A No. Turn it off, excuse yourself, and check frequently for messages outside of the room where you can return the call in private.

showed poor manners and a lack of common courtesy.

Etiquette is just plain good manners, common courtesy. Successful business relationships, just like successful personal relationships, rely on common courtesy. In this chapter we will take a look at some rules of etiquette that relate to networking activities but which should be remembered and observed in any business situation.

Most of us learned the rules of etiquette as we grew up—from our parents, school, peers, mentors, and sometimes from observation. A friend told me a story how as a young department store buyer on her first trip to Europe, she attended an elegant dinner party at the Florentine villa of the owner of a knitwear manufacturer with whom her store did business. She had never been to such an event, and learned to survive by close observation of the manners of others at the party. While it worked in this situation, you can't always rely on observation to learn the rules of etiquette. This chapter has some etiquette tips and techniques to help you out in most networking and business situations.

Here are some common networking situations and rules of etiquette for each.

At a Networking Event or Meeting

1. Arrive on time or even early. A late arrival at a meeting shows disrespect. It signals you think your time is more valuable than the time of those at the meeting. An early arrival shows enthusiasm for the event and respect for other people's time. (An added benefit is that an early arrival gives you control over who you want to meet.)

2. Place your nametag on your right-hand lapel. This places it in direct eye contact of the person you meet. This allows others to see who you are and to remember your name.

3. Exchange business cards with ease. Place

Q I'm going to a networking event and have been advised to hand out at least twenty-five business cards. Is this a good goal?

A A better goal is to make a certain number of quality contacts and to follow up after the meeting. Just handing your card does not mean you have made a connection.

Q I'm looking for a new job. Should I send a mass e-mail to my contact list asking for referrals?

A No. Thoughtfully go through your list and send a personalized message, or make a phone call.

Q I'm trying to get business from a company. I know that a friend of a contact of mine knows the president. Should I use that person's name when calling for an appointment?

A Only if you have permission from both parties—your contact and his friend. Then be sure to send a thank-you note to each.

your cards in your right-hand jacket pocket where you can easily access them. Make sure you have enough to last through the event. Make sure they are fresh, and do not look like they have been collecting lint in your pocket. Place cards you receive from those you meet in your left-hand pocket. This way you will not inadvertently give out someone else's card, thinking it is your own.

4. Make eye contact and keep it. Looking someone in the eye shows respect. People can tell when your eyes are wandering over the room looking for your next contact.

5. Shake hands firmly. There is nothing worse than a "fishy" or "death grip" handshake. Make your handshake firm and professional.

6. Be aware of personal space. Don't get too close. It causes discomfort. Anything closer than eighteen inches is considered too close by most people.

7. Welcome others into your conversation with grace. Extend your hand in welcome and be inclusive.

8. Exit a conversation politely. Express pleasure at having met the individual and hope that you will meet again (see "Have an Exit Strategy" from Chapter 2).

9. On eating and carrying on a conversation: Don't do it.

10. On drinking and carrying on a conversation: A non-alcoholic drink without ice is the easiest to handle. Why no ice? Frigid handshakes are not pleasant.

Meals—At Large Events Or Private Functions

1. Turn off your cell phone. Taking, or worse, making a call at a meal shows disrespect. It says, "The person I am speaking with is more important to me than you are."

2. First introduce yourself to the person seated to your right and your left. Then introduce yourself to the rest of the table. As others join your table, introduce yourself and others to them.

3. Wait for those at the head table to begin eating. Or, if at a private meal, wait for the host or hostess to begin. If you are the host or hostess, you must begin first.

4. When ordering, allow your guest to order first. Direct the server first to your guests. Then select your entrée accordingly. It is safest to pick something in the mid-price range.

5. If you don't know which utensil to use, working from the outside in is the safest bet. Alternatively, watch the host or hostess and do as they do.

6. Keep your napkin in your lap until you leave the event or restaurant. If you leave the table temporarily, leave the napkin on your chair.

7. Not sure which water glass or salad plate is yours? Remember liquids on the right, solids on the left. If your neighbor forgets and takes yours, just ignore it.

8. When you are finished, place your knife and fork in a parallel position

Remember, You are Always "On"

Shortly after getting settled on a flight from New York to LA, I smiled and said hello to my seatmate. As we began chatting we witnessed an unbelievable scene. The man across the aisle was sitting reading a paper when a passenger who had just boarded and was attempting to put his bags overhead said to him, "Hey, move your bags. You're taking up too much room." The first man looked at him with shock and said, "Sorry, but I only have one bag in the rack and I believe that is allowed." The second man started to get huffy and the flight attendant had to calm him down. Eventually he flopped down in his seat next to the first man

across the center of your plate. This signals the waiter to clear your setting.

9. Even if you are still hungry, stop eating when everyone else is done. Slow eaters beware. If it is that bad, get a snack later. Conversely, if you are a fast eater, slow your pace to match others.

10. Don't talk with your mouth full. Yes, I know. You learned this when you were six. At your next event, just watch how many folks still do this. Make sure you are not one of them.

11. Hold off talking about business until after the main course is removed. This allows ample time for small talk and getting acquainted. In addition, the servers will be out of the way.

12. Ask before you take notes. It is perfectly acceptable to take notes at a business or networking event, just ask first out of courtesy. Then use a small note pad, not an SUV-sized day planner.

13. Keep a mini etiquette survival kit with you. Include a note pad, several pens, business cards, Kleenex, hand wash sterilizer, comb and breath mints.

Making Introductions

1. In the business world, defer to position and age. Gender is not a factor. An introduction is normally made in a logical order:

- Introduce younger to older.
- Introduce your company peer to a peer in another company.
- Introduce a junior to a senior executive.
- Introduce a fellow executive to a client.
- Introduce a personal contact to a business contact. For example, my friend Judy accompanies me to an industry luncheon. We are seated with one of my clients. I would say, "(client), May I introduce my friend Judy? Judy, this is (client)." An easy way to remember how to do this is to always state the name

and continued to mutter under his breath and to be generally rude throughout the flight.

My seatmate leaned over to me and said, "That guy is being a real jerk! Most of us on this flight are going to the same conference and the man he is insulting happens to be the president of his company's largest account! There is a big dinner tonight where he will be sure to meet him." I wish I could have been a fly on the wall when the two came face-to-face under different circumstances. Good manners are not just for special occasions; remember, you are always on, so always watch your manners.

of the person you are making the introduction to first, and remember to introduce "to you," not "you to." "President Bush, I'd like to introduce my daughter, Sue, to you."

2. When making introductions, give a brief statement about each person's interest or profession, or better yet, something the two might have in common. This is polite and gets the conversation going.

E-mail Etiquette

E-mail makes our life easier. It is immediate, efficient, and convenient. It is a wonderful communication tool; however, sometimes your message can be misunderstood if you do not follow certain conventions. E-mail lacks the vocal inflections of a phone call, the body language of a face-to-face communication, and the impact of a handwritten note on fine stationary. Here are some e-mail etiquette tips:

1. Keep your e-mails brief and focused.

2. Use meaningful subject lines.

3. Use a format: purpose, body, and action.

4. If you need to send a long document, send it as an attachment.

5. Do not forward jokes, chain letters, warnings about viruses, or other junk mail that is making its rounds throughout the Internet. It is unprofessional and a waste of everyone's time.

6. Always re-read your message before you hit send. Make sure your tone is what you want it to be. Avoid anything that could be construed as sarcasm or innuendo.

7. Answer all e-mails within forty-eight hours. If you are going to be away from your computer, use the "away from my desk until..." message available in most e-mail programs.

Phone Etiquette

1. Return all phone calls within forty-eight hours.

2. When making a call, ask if it is a good time to talk, or when is, and follow their lead.

3. State the purpose of your call and indicate you would like a few minutes of their time. Do not take any longer.

4. When leaving a message, state your name, purpose, and action needed clearly and

When You Ask For Help Do It With Finesse

Last New Year's day I received an intriguing e-mail from someone I barely knew. The "To" box had my e-mail address plus about twenty others. In the subject box was written "Holiday Greetings." The sender had attached his resume to a greeting that read, "Dear Friend: Happy Holidays! I'm still looking for a job. Please forward my attached resume to all of your contacts A.S.A.P."

Amazing. I wonder how many people granted him the favor he asked. I was not one of them.

If you are going to send a "mass e-mail," use the tool in your e-mail software that makes your e-mail look like it is being sent only to the person who receives it. And learn the polite way to ask for a favor, as described later in this chapter.

A Word About Speakerphones

Speakerphones are another great modern convenience especially helpful when you need to include others in your conversation or if you need to move about the room while talking. However, these devices can be misused.

I have a friend in sales whose client always used a speakerphone. Apparently, he found it much easier to carry on a conversation when his hands were free. However, my friend had a big problem whenever she had to call him. She is a bit hard of hearing and the speakerphone echo was just enough to make it difficult for her to understand him. Although it was hard for her to say, she finally had to ask him to please pick up the phone so she could carry on a conversation.

When you find it necessary or convenient to use a speakerphone, always ask permission from the other party. In addition, when others are in the room, be sure to ask if it is OK to include them in the conversation and then be sure to make introductions.

succinctly. And most importantly, when leaving your phone number, speak slowly.

5. When calling a contact referral, state your name and who referred you. For example, "Hello (name), my name is Andrea Nierenberg. (so and so) suggested I give you call about...."

6. Don't multi-task while on the phone. People can hear you typing on your computer or shuffling papers. This shows you are not focused on them. Remember, "To do two things at once is to do neither."

The Right Way to Ask for A Favor

When you have been a good resource to others (see Chapter 7) it is easy to ask for a favor. Most people are happy to help, especially if you know how to ask. Here are some opening lines you could use:

■ "Perhaps you can help me...."

- "Who do you know that...?"

- "Who would you feel comfortable referring me to?"

- "I'd like to get your advice on...."

- "Maybe you could steer me in the right direction...."

- "If you were in my shoes, what would be your next step?"

Always remember to say thank you with an e-mail, hand-written note, or a gift.

Following Up

Following up is good networking etiquette.

1. Always send a thank-you note or an e-mail within forty-eight hours after a meeting. Thank your contact for his or her time and consideration and confirm any follow-up steps.

2. Get permission for "next steps." Ask when is a good time to call or get together. Also ask, "What is the best way for us to keep in touch (e-mail, phone, or plan a face-to-face meeting)?" These steps show respect for the other person's time and preferences.

3. Be sure to follow up when asked specifically for a referral, materials, your resume, or other resource information. Ask, "When do you need this?" and then send it on time (or earlier).

Here is another example of negative networking I observed on a flight to a convention. The saga began during the boarding process as a man stopped in the aisle to say something to a passenger already seated. The other passengers piled up behind him as he introduced himself and began a long presentation. Apparently, the gentleman to whom he was giving his "pitch" was an executive whom he recognized but did not know personally. The poor man was captive. He politely smiled as passengers squeezed by this fellow who just kept on talking! He finally

Networking At Non-Networking Events

Networking, if you think of it as connecting, learning about and helping others, and building relationships can be done anywhere, anytime. However, remember how inappropriately our friend the stockbroker acted at the wedding? Had he been at a networking meeting instead of at a wedding reception, his actions may have seemed perfectly appropriate. The purpose of a networking meeting is to share information and to ask for referrals. The purpose of a wedding reception is to celebrate. Does this mean you should not meet people at such functions and begin to establish relationships? Of course not. However, the proper way to do this at social events and other non-networking events is with discretion.

1. Recognize where you are and what you are there for.

2. When you come across a potential business contact, graciously suggest,

"Perhaps this is not a good time to discuss business, so may I give you a call on (date) and we could discuss this further, (consider some options), (I could help you out)?"

3. Ask permission before exchanging business cards. Then the exchange of cards should be as discreet as handing a tip to a maitre'd.

4. Recognize that there are establishments, such as some private clubs, where the conducting of business is simply not allowed. Be aware of where you are and follow the prescribed behavior.

had to sit down, yet at least twice during the two-hour flight he came back to drop off what appeared to be his resume and other materials and to continue his pitch.

I was seated across the aisle from this scene and could obviously tell from the executive's body language that this fellow was not making a favorable impression. I'm sure the fellow making his pitch was excited to have the opportunity to meet this executive, but he would have made a better impression had he introduced himself in the boarding area and then asked permission to send his materials as a follow-up.

Keeping Score

For some folks, networking means that if you do someone a favor, a favor is owed you in return. It is almost as if they keep a scorecard for every contact. Personally, I believe in just helping others, and if I receive something in

**Five Things Effective
Networkers Always Do:**

1. Show respect for other
people's time
2. Offer to help others
3. Show appreciation
4. Share information
5. Follow up

return, I consider it a gift, not a right. Here is my advice on "keeping score."

1. Always return a favor given to you.

2. Don't expect, or demand, a favor be returned to you.

3. Give only for the sake of giving.

In Summary

This chapter has stressed the importance of etiquette in networking. Networking and good manners are compatible. Networking is about building relationships with others, and as in any relationship, common courtesy counts.

Are you wondering how to keep track of all the contacts and information you are gathering as you master the networking process? In the next chapter I'll tell you how I organize and keep track of over 2,500 contacts in my network.

Chapter 9

Organizing and Keeping Track Of Your Network

Don't expect this chapter to be full of high-tech jargon and recommendations for state-of-the-art computer hardware and software. My theory is that your system should be simple, flexible, and easy to use—KISS. (Keep It Simple, Sweetheart.) My system for organizing and keeping track of a network database will work just as well if you use handwritten 3- x -5 cards as it will with the latest hand-held PDA (personal digital assistant). Whlle I use Microsoft Outlook to store and organize my network database, you could just as easily use Lotus Notes or a contact management application such as Act or Goldmine if you are already familiar with it. If you use America Online, the address book in AOL 7.0 can be used for your network database.

Keep in mind that whatever system you use—from stapling business cards to a

Rolodex card to the latest software available—make it work for you and use it consistently. Your system should work for you; you should not have to work for your system. The master networkers live by this. The information they need is always at hand because their system is organized and accessible. Take the time to set up a system and then make sure you keep it up.

Setting Up a Database

Here's how I set up my database with MS Outlook. First, I enter contact information: name, title, company, address, phone, fax, cell phone, and e-mail. Then I enter my contact's preferred method of communication: E for e-mail, V for voice mail (phone) right by their name. Other information I know about them goes in the "details" section. Then in the "activities" section (which is really like a large notepad) I enter the information I want to remind myself about in the future such as: work-related information, personal interests, what food they like, what books they like, a favorite restaurant, sports activities, and family information including names of spouse and children. Back in the "general" section, I click on the "categories" tab to select categories for this contact. I add categories as necessary. Here are some that I use:

- Client, prospect, supplier, professional, or personal
- "Hot" contact?—need to follow up more frequently
- Source of contact—referral, organization, event, meeting, etc.

- Ideas and referrals they have given me—including thank-you chain contacts

- Gift history—gifts and premiums sent, date, occasion

- Holiday cards sent

- A, B, and C (my way of prioritizing contacts, see Chapter 7)

These categories are useful when I want to sort or print my contact list by category.

Birthday List

Remember the birthday cards I mentioned in Chapter 7? I keep track of them by adding the contact's name to my birthday list after I enter basic information into the database. This list is a simple Word document file folder with each month being a separate document. I enter only the name in the document that is the month of the contact's birthday. Then, once a month, I print the list for that month, look up addresses for each person on the list, and mail each a birthday card. I've heard there are software programs that do this for you, but this "low tech" system is easy and efficient enough for me.

Business Cards

The more you network, the more business cards you will collect. You will want to have a system to capture and keep the information and to file the card. Here is my system. As soon as I return to my office from an event, I immediately scan the card into my database. (A business card scanner is a handy device for an active networker.) Then I enter the notes I have written about them into the activities section, along with follow-up tasks and dates. If the contact is going to become a client, prospect, or other active contact, I staple the card to a file folder in which I will file materials and other information. Since these contacts will be active, I want the card for easy access when I pick up the folder either in the office or on the road.

All other cards get put into the circular file next to my desk. I have already captured the information in my database and I don't like clutter.

Keeping Track of Conversations and Meetings

I take notes on all the conversations I have. Besides helping to keep facts straight about business matters, important follow-up tasks and dates, it also is a reminder about any personal information that is mentioned—a new grandchild, an upcoming family celebration, a favorite team or sporting event. These notes give me conversation starters for the next time we meet, as well as reminders to send a note. When I get back to my computer, I record my notes in the "activities" section of the contact's record in my database including the date, purpose of the meeting, highlights of our discussions, and follow-up tasks and dates. Besides entering follow-up dates here, I also enter them in my day planner (more on day planners later).

I do have a Palm OS (operating system) PDA (personal digital assistant), so I sync (transfer) all of my database information at least once a week or more often depending upon need.

Staying Up-to-Date and Organized on the Road

I travel a lot, for both business and pleasure. It is important to me to keep in touch no matter where I am in the world. So I carry my network with me with the help of portable devices, both high-tech, and low-tech. In addition to my laptop computer, I carry a PDA, a cell phone, and a day planner everywhere I go.

Using a Palm OS-PDA (Personal Digital Assistant)

These handy devices come in all shapes, sizes, and prices. Like any other device, such as a computer or a digital camera, you have to decide how you will use the device before you invest.

Gina, A New Contact

Here is how I followed up with Gina, a new contact I met at an association meeting:

1. Recorded the information from her business card into my contact database.
2. Wrote the date, event, and association where we met.
3. Recorded in my notes that she owned her own business, had one daughter, and lived in New Jersey.
4. Made notes about our conversation.
5. Sent her a "nice to meet you note" and my newsletter.
6. Marked down in my day planner to call Gina in two weeks for a follow-up meeting.

Personally, I use my PDA only to have my database (contact information and notes) with me. My PDA is not wireless—I can access my e-mail from any computer so I don't need this feature. I do not use the calendar, although, if I did it would eliminate having to carry a day planner with me. This is my personal preference. Do what is best for you.

The ability to access contact information and notes for every person in my network is invaluable to me. I use MS Outlook for my contact database and all Palm OS hand-held devices will transfer information from and to a computer with this software using a process called syncing. It is easy. You can also transfer information from Lotus Notes and several other contact management software programs. Check your PDA's manual. Note: As of the writing of this book, Palm OS devices do not sync information from AOL's Address Book. If you use this system, you need to install additional software on your PDA.

Day Planners

As noted, I do not use the calendar function on my PDA, or on my computer for that matter. I carry a day planner, a red leather Filofax. I like it for several reasons: it is handy, it looks professional, and it is pretty. (Okay, enough of the image thing.) Here is how I use my day planner:

◾ As a calendar—for appointments, follow-up reminders, important dates.

- For taking notes—at meetings, of telephone conversations, for general notes to myself.

- As an address book—for my most important and current contacts.

- To hold things—business cards, note cards, stamps, pictures of my family.

Again, it is my personal preference to carry a day planner. Certainly in this day and age, you can use the calendar on your computer that you can sync to your PDA if you find that more efficient. Remember, whatever system you use, keep it up-to-date and be consistent.

Cell Phones

My cell phone is always with me. I store important contact numbers in its memory so I can make quick calls. For all other numbers, I consult my PDA. There are devices on the market now that combine PDA and cell phone functions. Someday maybe I will invest in one, but for now my system works just fine for me.

Some other pointers about cell phones:

- Always have it with you.

- Use the voice mail system, retrieve messages frequently, and return calls promptly.

- Turn it off in restaurants, meetings, or other places where it would disturb others.

Even when I am away from the office and involved in a project or workshop, I make it a point to keep in touch and keep up my network database. Here is how I did this one day while on a business trip to Washington, DC.

During breaks in the day:

1. I checked messages. (There were seventeen.)
2. I left ten voice mail messages immediately. I returned the others within twenty-four hours.
3. Checked and returned e-mails. (I did this twice, during breaks.)
4. I called back a newspaper reporter and did a ten minute interview. In the course of our conversation I found out information about him: name, e-mail address, how long he had worked for his paper, where he was

▪ Use it to leave voice messages to your-self to follow up when you return to your office.

Keeping Your System Current and Keeping in Touch

I set aside a block of time to review my contact list every month. My review usually takes about four hours total, and I try to break it up into smaller blocks of time. First, I review every contact record, making sure it is up-to-date and making any category changes that are neces-sary. Then I print out the records for each of my A and B contacts. From this, I make a contact plan for the month. I determine who I need to contact, why, and when, and I mark it on my calendar. My goal is to list at least three people to contact everyday for the next month.

As I add new people to my database, I always send them a "nice to meet you" note and a copy of my newsletter within 24 hours. Another regular task is recording information from meetings, conversations, and follow-up tasks. Follow-up dates and tasks are recorded on my calendar and become a part of my daily "to do" list along with contacting the three people I have noted from my monthly review as well as any birthday or special event cards I have noted to send.

Managing E-mail

What did we do before we had e-mail? It is certainly an efficient and effective way to keep in touch and even to network. (See Chapter 8.) But for some people, it can be hard to manage. If you are an active networker and business professional, you will get lots of e-mails every day. Here is how I manage my e-mail correspondence.

■ Check e-mails frequently, throughout the day.

from, what kind of note paper he used (the interview was about sending notes), and his favorite hotel and restaurant (even a favorite dish) in Washington. I also learned that I had been referred to him by his managing editor who had interviewed me in the past.

I wrote all of this down in my day planner. When I returned to my office that evening, I did the following:

1. Sent him a handwritten note.
2. Sent his managing editor a note to say thank you for the referral.
3. Entered all of his information into my database.
4. Sent him a copy of my latest newsletter.

A week later, he called me for an interview on another article he was writing.

Trivia Games Can Help You Organize Your Database

A friend, Robert, shared with me how he organizes his network: "I loved trivia games when I was a kid, especially Trivial Pursuit. I excelled at remembering weird facts about geography, history, and sports. For me, one of the most important aspects of networking is knowing all kinds of things about the people in my network. I remember details about my friends and colleagues, from the most basic (i.e. names of children) to the more esoteric (i.e. classes that my roommate took in college). As soon as possible after I meet with someone, I write down everything I can remember about the interaction.

- Return all e-mails within 24 hours (48 hours is considered acceptable).
- I try to send a response immediately, even just to say "I received your e-mail and will get back to you...."
- Keep e-mails short and to the point.

MS Outlook and other e-mail systems have a feature that allows you to access your e-mail even when you are away from your office or home computer. Even if I don't have my laptop with me, I will stop at a Kinko's, a hotel business center, or ask to use a client's computer wherever I am in the world and return my e-mails. This is not only a good follow-up habit, but it takes only minutes if you do it everyday as opposed to hours if you wait until you return to your office.

In Summary

No matter how you choose to organize your list and information, the important thing is to have a system and use it. A key to successful networking is follow-up. Having a well-organized and up-to-date database and a system to access it will help you do this.

In Chapter 10 we will take a look at the plans, commitments, and success of some folks like you who have used nonstop networking techniques to achieve goals and dreams in their lives. This will tie it all together for you.

During a game of Trivial Pursuit, you would never be allowed to look up answers in an encyclopedia or on the Internet. With networking, you're encouraged not to rely on your memory but to use a contact database of some sort to organize your information. (Note: I use a product called InfoGenie2, a free-form database as opposed to a "field-based" database.)

In Trivial Pursuit, if you know the right information, you can get a "pie wedge" for your playing piece. In networking, if you know the right information, you amaze your friends and gain esteem from them—much more so than if you beat them in a game of Trivial Pursuit! In short, networking is anything but a trivial pursuit!"

Chapter 10

Tying It All Together

I am always amazed and delighted when the phone rings and someone says to me, "Andrea, you're right—these techniques really do work and let me tell you what happened." Out comes a success story about a new job, new career, contract won, or a new relationship. Sometimes it is a story about newfound confidence in the ability to meet people and make connections. Most gratifying are the many letters and e-mails I receive where people say their lives have been transformed because they made networking a part of their everyday lives.

By now, I hope that you, too, are benefiting from the principles and techniques of *Nonstop Networking*. You can incorporate every single thing we have talked about in each chapter—from attitude and techniques to continuity and organization—into your daily life starting today.

- Attitude—That networking is a lifelong process.

- Techniques—You have all the techniques at hand to make it happen.

- People—Every contact you make is the chance to learn something new.

- Organization—Keeping contacts and information at your fingertips is easy.

Attitude Is Everything

When we started our journey together, we saw how a negative attitude could stop us from networking, even when we realized how important this skill was to our success. Yet, when you give yourself permission to network, and change from a negative to a positive outlook, good things begin to happen.

A Photographer's Story

My friend the photographer had this to say: "Andrea, what do you mean, the opposite of networking is <u>not</u> working? That does not make sense to me. It seems to me networking is not only work, it is hard work." What Andrea meant, she explained, was that when you are not networking, you are simply not working. Or, to carry it further, you are just standing still in life. Like I was—afraid to get out there and network to get clients and start my business.

"Take baby steps," she urged. "Plan what you will say when you meet someone new. Develop a 30-second infomercial about yourself. Go through your address books and re-connect with some old friends and colleagues."

I did. The more I did it, the better I became at these skills. Actually, it wasn't as though I was not good at it in the first place. I like meeting people. It was just that I had a bad attitude about "networking."

What happened was an epiphany of sorts. I stopped thinking about myself and networking for my business and focused on the people I was meeting and re-connecting with. As Andrea suggested, I looked for ways to be a resource and to make connections. I love to entertain, so I put together a series of dinner parties where I concentrated on putting together people I thought would enjoy meeting one another. I also hosted a number of neighborhood get-togethers. I recall remarking to my husband after one such event, "We are so fortunate to have such interesting neighbors, from all walks of life."

My network expanded as I continued to meet people and to re-connect with those I had lost touch with. I was having fun! And my business got off the ground. My 30-second infomercial was effective—I think mostly because I am so enthusiastic about my new profession. Also, everyone has something to say about photography, and almost everyone needs a portrait of themselves, a family member, a pet, or even of their house. I see now what Andrea means when she says that every single person we meet is someone we have an opportunity to learn from. Everyone has something to offer, and who knows—that person may turn out to be a potential client for you.

My business is still young. But all of the clients I have so far have come from networking efforts. The amazing thing is I don't think of it as networking. It is just meeting people and talking about something I love to do!

Armed with Your Arsenal

You have all the techniques at hand to make it happen. You can use them at any event or in any situation that arises. To use them effectively, just remember the following:

- Know who you are
- Focus on others
- Have a goal

Know who you are. How do you want people to remember you? It is more than your business card; it is the line that makes someone say, "Oh, really—how do you do that?" It is the description of yourself delivered with natural enthusiasm and, yes, even with passion.

Focus on others. Keep your "conversation starter" and "get to know you" questions fresh and timely. Practice them and watch how your conversations become easier and more interesting. Your goal is to get others talking about themselves so that you can learn their needs and how you can be a resource for them.

Have a goal. Networking is a life-long process; however, your networking goals will change throughout your life. At any given time, you may be more or less concerned with the following:

- Finding a new job
- Getting a promotion
- A career change
- Finding a life partner
- A new business venture
- Clients for your business
- Political aspirations
- Personal interests
- A lifestyle change
- Moving to a new location

Armed with the techniques from this book, you can accomplish your goals in any of these areas.

Deborah's Story

My friend Deborah, a vice-president of an advertising agency, told me how she found her life partner by setting a goal and using networking techniques. (I've changed names and some details in this story to protect the privacy of the parties involved.)

First Deborah wrote out exactly what she was looking for in a life partner. For starters, he had to be a certain age, religion, and come from a background similar to hers. He had to have many of the same interests she did, including a zest for travel. Most importantly, she was looking for someone who shared her values and goals, especially about raising a family.

Then she identified the places where she would likely meet such a person. She joined specific business and social interest groups, she got more involved in her church, and she taught a course at a local community college. She joined the board of a local non-profit group and volunteered to chair an event. She also began networking at her health club. Deborah was just living her life. She joined and got involved with things that interested her, but with a specific goal of making contacts, knowing that one of these contacts might turn out to be, or lead her to, her life partner.

She also, however subtly, told others about her goal. In business terms, she asked for referrals. Ultimately, that is how she met Doug, whom she married a year ago. Along the way, she met many interesting people, dated several prospective life partners, made some beneficial business contacts, and found some lifelong friends. She tells me she also fine-tuned her networking techniques, which have served her well in a subsequent job search.

Identify and Expand

Every contact you meet is the chance to learn something new. Keep identifying these people and the places they gather. Build on your current database of contacts and seek out new ones. These contacts enrich your life and lead you to relationships that help you achieve your life's goals.

Networking Plan for a Public Relations Agency

My friend and publicist, Tom, successfully incorporated a networking plan into his business plan. This has helped him stay on track to expand his network and to grow his business.

"Before I opened a new office in downtown Chicago for my growing public relations firm, I wrote a business plan that included a networking strategy. I had been working with Andrea for a number of years, and she had not only taught me the techniques of networking, but I knew from first-hand observation of the growth of her business that they worked.

"Since a key aspect of public relations is building relationships with the media, the first thing I did was find a location close to the offices of every major national and local media outlet in Chicago. I did this for convenience and visibility for my firm. Then, after attending a couple of meetings and meeting some people, I joined two key networking organiza-tions: the Chicagoland Chamber of Commerce and the Central Michigan Avenue Association. Both of these organizations provide opportunities to network with businesses that need to get their names in the media.

"At the beginning of each month, I make a specific networking plan. I look at three important areas from which to choose my networking activities: what organization events and meetings I can attend; what upcoming meetings and conventions listed in the business press would be worthwhile; and lastly, which TV or radio producer or reporter contacts of mine I should arrange to meet this month. I make the calls, mark dates on my calendar, and follow up.

"The meetings I set up with my media contacts are in addition to ones where I am pitching a particular client or a story. I simply try to learn more about my contact and his publication. This strategy makes it easier to connect when I do want to pitch a client or a story. While most of the time these meetings are just for gathering information and staying in touch, sometimes they lead to bigger opportunities.

"One time while I was having lunch with the editor of a national business publication, he asked me if I could recommend someone for a panel on business-to-business Internet marketing. I helped him out by introducing him to a contact of mine who was a marketing manager for a national wireless phone company. It was a networking win for me for two reasons: First, I became a resource for the editor, and second, it gave me a reason to re-connect with my contact at the wireless phone company, so I could keep my name in front of him. Subsequently, I've had the opportunity to meet with him to discuss future business.

"Another part of my networking plan involves day-to-day contacts. I learned from Andrea's advice to network everywhere, even in your elevator. For example, when I am alone with someone in the elevator on the way up to my office and the other person is getting off on a different floor, I sometimes say, "Hi, may I ask what you do on ...floor?" So far, I have made connections with a graphics design agency and a national investment firm. I just keep identifying and expanding my contacts, and my business keeps on growing."

Organize It All with a K.I.S.S.

Develop a simple system for keeping your contact information readily available. I described how I use Microsoft Outlook with a PDA, a day planner, and a cell phone. It works, because I work at keeping it current and accessible. Find and use a system that works for you.

If you connect with just four people a week ("**Four**-mula for success") you'll be using a system that puts you ahead of most people who say they are networkers. Every week, just call, e-mail, or write a note to:

1. A client or prospect (remember, we are all in sales)

2. A former colleague

3. A former friend or associate

4. A current friend

It couldn't be more simple than this!

It's a Forever Process

I'll always remember with a smile one of my seminar participants named

Bill. A very likeable and interesting man, he actively participated and seemed to enjoy the session. At the end, he came up and made a shocking observation. "Andrea," he said, "I tried all of this networking nonsense for about three months and then I stopped because nothing happened." I looked at him quizzically and said, "Bill, what exactly did you expect to happen in three short months?" Networking is about building relationships that are mutually beneficial to both parties over time. Sometimes you get benefits immediately; other times it may be years. There is no timetable; it is a lifetime process.

Doors do open a lot easier than they once did for me. I know this is because networking, as I have described it in this book, is a way of life for me. It is a forever process—nonstop networking.

Throughout this book and in my seminars, I stress the importance of being a resource to others, showing appreciation, and following up. When you continually incorporate those three small steps into your everyday life you will build the relationships that will help you achieve success in life.

Thank you for taking the time to learn and adapt some of these principles and techniques into your life. I would like to know how they work for you. Feel free to drop me a note, an e-mail, or give a call. You know I'll follow up!

Good luck and all best wishes for your continued success!

52 Nonstop Networking Tips

1. Give yourself permission to network. Changing your attitude to a positive one is the first step to networking success.

2. Make a list of opening lines to use when meeting someone new. Use open-ended questions that require more than a one-word answer, or at least follow up with an open-ended question.

3. Develop a 30-second infomercial about yourself. Practice it until it becomes spontaneous and natural.

4. Do your research before attending an event. Learn the basics about the organization and the people likely to be at the event.

5. Have a list of "get to know you" questions. These go deeper than opening line questions; they help you to know the interests of the person you have just met.

6. Keep a journal of small talk topics. These include current events, industry topics, books and movies, community topics, and the like.

7. Set a goal for every event or meeting you attend. A good goal is to meet two new people, make a connection, and send a follow-up note, call, or e-mail.

8. Smile when meeting people, entering a room, or talking on the phone. A smile is the first step in building rapport.

9. Look the other person in the eye. Eye contact says you are focused on the conversation and interested in what the other person is saying.

10. Listen with care. Be aware of what the other person is saying instead of thinking about what you will say next. You will remember much more about the person and the conversation.

11. Learn to remember names. This skill will set you apart from many. Listen carefully when the name is said, repeat it frequently, and create a mind picture that will help you associate the person with the name.

12. Give compliments. Make a goal to look for positive attributes and give five compliments a day.

13. Make a list of the key people in your industry or profession that you would like to meet. Determine what organizations, places, and people they know to help you find a way to meet them.

14. Re-connect with four people a week. This week call a client or prospect you have not been in touch with for a while, a former business colleague, a former friend, and a current friend you haven't spoken with for a while.

15. Join a networking group such as BNI or Leads Club and go to the meetings. Even if you don't get any referrals, it is a good way to practice networking techniques such as your 30-second infomercial.

16. Research and join an industry or professional group. Go to two meetings, meet two people, and set up two follow-up meetings before you make your decision to join.

17. Join a service group, such as a Chamber of Commerce or a fund-raising organization. Follow your interests in this matter. Join for the sake of giving, not getting.

18. Follow your interest and take a class, join a health club, take a cruise. Remember, you need like-minded people in your network.

19. Volunteer, write an article, or join a committee in your organization. Becoming known helps you meet people and develop relationships faster and more profitably than just attending meetings.

20. Send three handwritten notes a day. Send these to people in your network to say thank you, offer congratulations, send an article of interest, extend an invitation, or just to keep in touch. Use "found time" during the day to write these notes, and make them short and simple. Carry note cards and stamps with you.

21. Write an article or newsletter to send to your contacts. This promotes your business and helps you keep in touch with your contacts. You can easily do this electronically.

22. Send gifts. Remember those who help you, or just remember a special occasion for those in your network. Develop a list of reliable vendors of unique gift items for these occasions.

23. Use premiums that constantly remind the recipients of your name and your business. Look for useful items that will be appreciated and that will keep your name in front of others.

24. Follow up within twenty-four hours of a meeting to say, "nice to meet you," "thanks for your time and consideration," and to set another meeting.

25. Call within two weeks of suggesting another meeting. "Let's do lunch" is not an effective networking technique. Make it happen.

26. Send the materials or information you promised on time or sooner than promised.

27. Thank your contact for a referral and let them know what happened.

28. Become a resource for others. Give generously of your time and expertise.

29. Look for unique and creative ways to have "face time" with others. Try having coffee, afternoon tea, taking a walk or run, getting a manicure, shopping, meeting at the sky club between flights, or meeting at an art gallery.

30. Remember birthdays and send cards. Find out the birthday month of each of your contacts, make a list of contacts by birthday month, and send out cards once a month to those on the month's list.

31. Develop a system to keep in touch with everyone in your network on a regular basis. As your list grows, divide it into categories and have a contact plan for each category.

32. Review your list on a regular basis and "clean out" those contacts who for whatever reason are no longer in your life.

33. Develop and maintain a database of your contacts. It need not be high-tech; it can be on 3- x -5 index cards. Your system should work for you; you should not have to work for your system.

34. Collect information about each contact besides the basic contact information. This includes interests, family, awards and promotions, special dates, how you met, and other pertinent facts.

35. Determine the way each contact prefers to communicate: by phone, e-mail, or in person. Note this on your database record.

36. Make and keep notes about each meeting with each contact. Refer to these when following up or before you next meet.

37. Have a system for filing business cards. As an active networker, you will collect many. Enter the information into your network database and then file the card depending upon how you plan to use it in the future.

38. Enter information about a new contact and follow up within 24 hours of your meeting.

39. Answer your phone and e-mail messages within 24 hours even when you are on the road. With today's modern technology, there is no reason not to be in touch.

40. If you are out of touch for a period, let people know with a message on your phone and an automatic e-mail message.

41. Everyday, send an email to someone in your Internet address book you have not heard from recently.

42. Once a week, go through your contact list and call three people just to say "hello."

43. Once a month, have lunch with a friend, colleague, or client you have not seen for a while.

44. At a company function, set a goal to sit next to someone new and get to know him or her.

45. When making telephone calls is uncomfortable, use a script and practice until it comes naturally.

46. Begin with a compliment. This is a wonderful way to start a conversation when you may not know what to say to break the ice.

47. When a conversation gets off the topic you want to talk about, use a "bridge" such as "that reminds me of..." to get back to your topic.

48. Attend meetings with a purpose. Have a specific goal in mind when attending an industry event or other networking meeting. It could be just to meet the speaker or someone else you know will be there.

49. Set a time limit. When spending an entire meeting with a group of strangers seems daunting, give yourself permission to leave after a specific time, say one hour.

50. When eye contact is difficult, set your gaze at the "third eye" —a spot just above the bridge of the nose between the eyes.

51. Network on the Internet. Online networking is a new and efficient way to establish relationships with those in your field.

52. Give yourself a reward for networking success—whether for attending an event for an hour, or landing a new job as a result of a networking contact. You deserve it!

Sample Notes

#1: The "Thank-You" Note

PURPOSE: Everyone wants to be appreciated. Whether you choose a handwritten note or an e-mail, make your "thank-you" notes sincere and specific. For example:

TEXT:

Dear Bob,

It was great to meet you last night at the chamber meeting. I really enjoyed what you shared about new risks in the stock market. Thanks for that great advice; it is most helpful.

Sincerely,

Susan Day

#2: Sharing Valuable Information

PURPOSE: It's important to stay connected with others by being a good source of information. When you meet someone new, make a note of what's important to him or her and then send that person information he or she would appreciate. Here's how:

TEXT:

Dear Mr. Walker:

I hope all is going well at your law firm. Enclosed is a magazine article about new ways law firms are finding new clients. Perhaps you'll find it helpful.

Best regards

Thomas Preston

#3: Planting Seeds for Future Meetings

PURPOSE: When we connect with people we want to meet again, it requires us to be proactive. Think about fun and creative ways to connect with another person and take the initiative. Try something like this:

TEXT:

Greetings Judy,

How are you? I remember when you shared that you are a big fan of artistic photography. There's a new contemporary photography exhibit at the Art Institute. A copy of the "members only" preview invitation is enclosed. Would you like to come as my guest?

Sincerely,

Ricky Chessman

(With this note be sure to make a follow-up call a few days later.)

#4: Connecting Your Contacts with Each Other

PURPOSE: Give and it will come back to you. If you know two people who could benefit from knowing each other, then help them connect. It's another way for you to stay connected to each of them and show that you are a valuable resource. Here's a note for this idea.

TEXT:

Dear Phil,

I was thinking about you and it came to mind that you were having trouble finding a reliable trucking service. I know a company that provides great trucking services for top companies. Enclosed is a business card for Bob Green, my contact there. Feel free to drop my name if you call.

Best regards,

David Simpson

Note to the person being referred:

Dear Bob,

I know someone who could use your trucking services. He has been disappointed so many times in the past with other companies. His name is Philip Stone and his card is enclosed. You might want to give him a call and say I referred you to him. I hope all is well.

Take care,

David Simpson

#5: Show appreciation to people you've never met

PURPOSE: Making new connections with people can be done in ways other than face-to-face. If you attended a trade show and were impressed with how well it was produced, then consider sending a note to the show's producer even if you never meet. Try something like this:

TEXT:

Dear Ms. Johnson:

I attended the booksellers' conference you produced in New York last week. I have gone to shows like it for ten years, and what you accomplished was the best trade event I ever attended. Congratulations on a job very well done!

Sincerely,

Patricia Fleming

#6: Remember Important Dates

PURPOSE: Everyone has a birthday, anniversaries, and special dates that they want to be remembered. Use your data organization system to keep track of these special dates and send out the appropriate cards. While cards for these types of occasions are readily available, consider either customizing them with an added note or using a blank note card. Here's how:

TEXT:

Dear Michael,

Happy anniversary to your business! I remember when you shared you dream for opening your new company. Now it's five years later and you are growing by leaps and bounds. Congratulations!

Best regards,

Harry Williams

#7: Spread the Appreciation Around

PURPOSE: Sometimes we can overlook a key contact that helped us make an important connection with someone. Perhaps because an executive assistant re-arranged his supervisor's schedule you got an appointment that would not have happened. Here's an example of how to thank these people:

TEXT:

Dear Robert,

I want you to know how much I appreciated you helping me secure an appointment with the president of your company. Without your assistance, I would never have gotten in to discover there was perfect match between our companies. When I come in next Tuesday for my 11:00 a.m. meeting, would you be able to go for lunch afterward?

Sincerely,

Martin Smith

#8: Connecting with a complete stranger

PURPOSE: Famous people in the newspapers are people too. And like anyone else they appreciate sincere notes. There is a pastor in Chicago who wrote to President Nixon saying that he was praying for him during the Watergate crisis. This lead to an ongoing exchange of letters.

Here's one illustration of connecting with people you have no connection with:

TEXT:

Dear Mr. Davis:

I read in the newspaper today about your company's efforts to crack down on low wage workers in your factories in other countries. You should be applauded for taking a proactive position even though your company was not under pressure to act. More corporate leaders should follow your example.

Sincerely,

Malcolm Forthright

Appendix 3

Resources for Cards, Gifts, and Premiums

Sending cards and giving gifts are effective ways to show appreciation and to stay in touch. Thoughtful cards and gifts are memorable and make you stand out. There are many companies that offer great items for this purpose. The following are a few of my favorite sources for unique and thoughtful ways to express your appreciation.

NAME: IntroKnocks
PHONE: 800-753-0590
WEB: www.introknocks.com

DESCRIPTION: IntroKnocks has several lines of business greetings cards that are unique from those available at most stationery stores. They even have a line of networking cards that offer a quick and effective way to follow up with people you meet through networking.

NAME: Fruition
PHONE: 800-481-3784
WEB: www.fruitiongifts.com

DESCRIPTION: Artfully packaged gifts of fresh fruit combined with yummy chocolate baked goods are a specialty of this delightful company. These folks even include a handwritten note with your message instead of the usual computer-generated card.

NAME: Colby Ridge: Popcorn & Gifts
PHONE: 800-328-2676
WEB: www.colbyridge.com

DESCRIPTION: Popcorn is a terrific thank-you gift that can be shared with others and is appreciated by all. There are two things I particularly like about Colby Ridge: Their popcorn is extra-fresh because it is popped shortly before being shipped, and they include a nice handwritten note with your message. Their attractive tins are always coveted as containers once the popcorn is gone.

171

NAME: Proflowers

PHONE: 1-888-373-7437

WEB: www.proflowers.com

DESCRIPTION: It is easy to order flowers from the Internet these days, but this unique company makes it even easier and the flowers come direct from the grower, ensuring a fresher, higher quality flower. Proflowers fulfillment system lets you know the status of your order by e-mail when your order is received, when the flowers are picked, when they are shipped, and finally, when they arrive at their destination. Cut flowers can come with their own vase, instructions for care, and a personalized note from you.

Personalized Gifts and Premiums

Coffee mugs, key chains, pens, magnets and other useful items make great gifts that keep your name in front of your contacts.

Finding sources for these can be a challenge because local Yellow Pages categorize them in so many different ways: advertising specialty items, corporate gifts, even trophies and awards. I recommend searching the Internet for "corporate gifts." Or, look in the resource guides in trade publications such as:

Incentive (www.incentivemag.com),

Potentials (www.potentialsmag.com),

Promotional Marketing (www.promotionalmktg.com).

Here are some tips for ordering personalized gift items:

1. **Ask for samples.** Most companies will send you free samples of the products you are considering.

2. **Ask which items are available in small quantities.** Prices for customized items are often quoted for large quantities. However, some are available in smaller quantities for a higher price. You just need to ask a sales representative.

3. **Ask to see a proof before your order is printed.** You will not only want to see how it is actually going to look, but you should proofread the copy. You do not want to give a gift with your name or company misspelled.

4. **Consider packaging.** Some items like coffee mugs and pens need a box or a uniquely sized envelope for shipping purposes. Be sure to ask if the supplier offers packaging to make it easier for you to ship these items.

Index

A
anniversaries, 109–110
appointments, telephone, 108
appreciation, 62–64, 111
articles, writing, 117
attitude, 153–155
    changing, 11
    positive, 8

B
baby steps, 56, 77–78, 84
birthdays, 109–110, 143
BNI. See Business Network International
body language, 27, 31–32
boundaries, 27, 32
bridging, 78
business cards
    handing out, 7
    magnetic, 119
    organizing, 141, 143–144
Business Network International (BNI), 93–96

C
caring, for others, 67–69
Carnegie, Dale (author), 30
cell phones, 147–148
clients, 38–40
comfort zone, 10
communication skills
    asking questions, 32–33
    giving compliments, 33–34
    listening, 29–30
    making eye contact, 28–29
    observing body language, 31–32
    remembering names, 30–31
    respecting boundaries, 32
    smiling, 27–28
communication styles, 58–59
competitors, 90–91
compliments
    as conversation starter, 78
    giving, 27, 33–34, 71
confidence, 54–56
connections
    creating, 5, 7

173

developing, 7
making, 6
conversations
  exiting, 130
  note taking during, 144–145
  starting, 7, 12, 23–24
  while eating and drinking, 130
correspondence, preferred method of, 109
customers, 38–40

D

databases, 3, 110
  maintaining, 148–149
  organizing, 8, 141–143
  setting up, 142–143
day planners, 146–147
dining etiquette, 131–133

E

effective networking, 140
elevators, 41
e-mail, 116, 134–135, 149–151
empathy, 56–58, 60–62
energy, 66–67, 82–83
enthusiasm, 16, 66–67
Epstein, Lee (godfather of direct marketing),
  96–97
etiquette
  dining, 131–133
  e-mail, 134–135
  networking, 8, 124–129, 137
  telephone appointments, 135–136
exit strategies, 7, 12, 24–25
extroverts, 71–72
eye contact, making, 27, 28–29, 79–81, 80–81,
  130

F

family, 46–47
Fishnets group, 94–95
follow-up, 6, 7, 78–79, 120–122, 137
Four-mula for Success, 92, 104, 160
friends, personal, 44–46

G

gifts, 171–172
  sending, 63, 110, 117–119
goals, 7, 12, 25–26
Google (internet search engine), 97
greeting cards, 114
groups, joining, 21–22

H

handshakes, 130
help, requesting, 135–137

I

infomercials, 30-second, 7, 11, 13–16
interests, in common, 27, 32–33
Internet, 16–17, 84–85
introductions, 11, 22–23, 131, 133–134
introverts, 7, 71–72, 74, 75

L

Leads Club, 93
Le Tip International, 93
listening, 6, 27, 29–30, 72–73
lists, 50–51, 89–91, 124–126, 143

M

meetings
  attending, 100–102
  chance, 43–44
  designated greeters, 11, 22
  with friends, 45
  for networking, 81–82
  one-on-one, 82, 123–124

N

NAFE. See National Assoc. of Female Executives
names, remembering, 27, 30–31
nametags, 28
National Assoc. of Female Executives (NAFE), 93
neighbors, 40–41
networker, effective, 69
networker, pathological, 68–69
networking
  action steps, 87–88
  basic theory of, 2–4
  effective networking, 140
  negative, 8, 69, 138–139
  non-stop, 5–6, 161
  reasons for avoiding, 3
  strategy, 104
networking etiquette, 8, 124–129, 137
networking events, 7, 11, 129–130
networking groups
  industry specific, 93, 96–97
  service groups, 98–99
  special interest, 93, 99–100
networks
  existing, 38
  expanding, 87–105, 100–105
newsletters, 103–105, 117

non-networking events, 138–139
notes
    hand-written, 62–64, 111, 115
    plan for sending, 114–116
    samples of, 113, 167–170
    sending, 44, 110, 137
    thank-you, 44, 62, 112
    types of, 113–114

O

opening lines, 11, 12, 17–19
organizations
    identifying, 92–93
    joining, 100–105

P

passion, 75
PDA. See personal digital assistants
people
    active, involved, 48–49
    ambitious, 48–49
    caring, 50
    happy, helpful, 48
    helping, 122, 139–140
    identifying, 88, 157
    learning about, 110–111
    like-minded, 41–43
    meeting, 6, 7
    meetings, 100–102, 155
    probing, 11
    types in network, 36–37
permission, giving yourself, 11
personal digital assistants, 141, 145–146
personality styles, 60–62
personal space, 130
phone calls, returning, 37
premiums, 118, 171–172
presentation skills, 105

Q

questions, 17–19
quiet networker
    goal setting, 76–77
    techniques for, 76–83

R

reconnecting, 91–92
referrals, 70–71
    asking for, 7
    contacting, 136
    developing, 94–95
    receiving, 43, 64, 121

relationships
    developing, 2, 5–6, 108, 111
    mutually beneficial, 47–50, 107
    nurturing, 5, 24
research, 11, 16–17
resources, 18, 171–172

S

scheduling, 83–84
schmoozing, 81–82
scripts, 78–79
seminars, 6–7
separation, six degrees of, 36–37
Shrout, Richard (indexer), 80–82
small talk, 11, 19–20
smiling, 27–28
speakerphones, 136
speakers, approaching, 22–23
speeches, 103–105
suppliers, 40

T

Tanquist, Stu (consultant), 83–84
techniques, twelve
    designated greeters, 22
    dinner partners, 23–24
    exit strategies, 24–25
    goals, 25–26
    infomercial, 30 second, 12–13
    introductions, 22–23
    joining, 21
    opening lines, 12–13
    questions, 17–19
    research, 16–17
    small talk, 19–20
    working a line, 20
telephone, 92, 108, 135–136
tenacity, 64–66
thank-you notes, 44, 62, 108, 112
The Wall Street Journal, 19
time limits, 83
topics, idea generating, 11, 19–20
traits, of great networkers, 57

V

volunteering, 102–103

W

waiting lines
    getting into, 11
    standing in, 20
word pictures, painting, 15

Leading companies count on Andrea Nierenberg for their training needs—sales, customer service, presentation skills, networking, and motivation.

POWERFUL PERSONAL MARKETING

Personal marketing skills contribute to our most rewarding professional relationships. Andrea's programs cover all aspects of effective networking and communication skills with sales leads, customers, and professional associates.

GREAT CUSTOMER SERVICE

Excellent customer service attracts customers and keeps them coming back. It's based on consistently using effective techniques, which Andrea knows how to create, present, and implement.

BETTER PRESENTATION SKILLS

Andrea's programs have helped thousands of business professionals, managers, and executives improve their presentation skills, strengthen their professional image, and enhance the appeal of the products and services they offer.

SUPERIOR SELF-MOTIVATION

An expert at getting people to accomplish more than they ever thought possible, Andrea's motivational programs have inspired professionals by helping them build confidence, become better leaders, and find greater satisfaction in their work and in their lives.

Call or e-mail today to find out about how The Nierenberg Group, Inc. can help you and your organization.   212-980-0930   andrean@selfmarketing.com

Visit our website and sign up for a FREE copy of our newsletter *The Nierenberg Report.* www.selfmarketing.com